English as an additional language (EAL) in practice

by Alice Bevan

Contents

Introduction	2
The national picture	4
The EYFS statutory framework	7
Chapter One EAL Essentials	11
What does EAL mean?	12
Groups of EAL learners	12
What is bilingualism?	13
Key EAL matters	15
Chapter Two How children learn languages	20
First language acquisition	21
Learning two languages simultaneously	23
Stages of additional language acquisition	24
Factors that impact additional language learning	26
Chapter Three Helping children to settle-in	31
Part A – Before the child starts	31
Part B – The child's first day	35
Part C – The child's first few weeks	38
Chapter Four Creating a suitable environment	41
Types of spaces within your setting	42
Types of materials and resources available	46
The familiarity and practicability of the setting	47
Chapter Five Adult-child interaction	52
Interacting with simultaneous learners (under 3 years)	55
Interacting with children who are new to English (sequential learners)	55
Interacting with a child during the 'silent period'	59
Providing opportunities for children to use their home language	59
The importance of play	62
Chapter Six Building positive relationships with parents and carers	64
General advice to promote good relationship building	65
Key messages to give to parents	70
Working with interpreters	72
Chapter Seven Observation, assessment and planning	73
Prime areas of learning and development and EAL learners	74
The characteristics of effective learning	74
Assessment requirements	77
Chapter Eight Working with children with communication difficulties	82
Understanding SLCN	84
Identifying SLCN in EAL learners	88
Supporting EAL learners with SLCN	92
Resources	96
Home activity sheets	96
Checklist for pre-start parent meeting	104
Checklist for determining abilities in a home language	106
Key words and phrases	108
References	112
Acknowledgements	116

Published by Practical Pre-School Books, A Division of MA Education Ltd, St Jude's Church, Dulwich Road, Herne Hill, London, SE24 0PB.
Tel: 020 7738 5244   www.practicalpreschoolbooks.com
Design: Mary Holmes fonthillcreative 01722 717036

© MA Education Ltd 2018. All images © MA Education Ltd. All rights reserved.

No part of this publication may be reproduced, stored in a retrieval system, or transmitted by any means, electronic, mechanical, photocopied or otherwise, without the prior permission of the publisher.

ISBN 978-1-909280-99-1

Introduction

'A child's experiences from birth to five have a major impact on their future life chances' (DfE, 2012).

This is true of all children, whether they are exposed to one language or to several languages; therefore it is essential that all early years settings are able to provide high quality learning experiences so that all children reach their full potential.

In some areas of the UK, a large proportion of the children attending early years settings speak a language other than English at home. Despite this high level of diversity, there continues to be a lack of clear guidance for early years practitioners on how to support children who are learning English as an additional language (EAL).

Research shows that many practitioners lack confidence in their knowledge of how best to support EAL learners (Murakami, 2008). Sood and Mistry (2015) found that 'practitioners wanted more awareness and training… in order to better support their EAL learners in their setting.' Murakami (2008) notes from her interview with one language support practitioner that 'everyone is just fumbling along' in meeting the needs of new EAL arrivals. This speaks volumes about the need for clear and comprehensive guidance, hence the reason for this book.

What's more, there are many myths and misconceptions about additional language learning (Conteh, 2015). These mixed messages make it hard for practitioners to feel confident in their ability to support EAL learners and to advise parents appropriately. This book aims to clarify the facts and ensure that any misconceptions held by readers are rectified, particularly in relation to supporting the communication and language development of EAL learners.

'Communication is the foundation of relationships and is essential for learning, play and social interaction' (The Communication Trust, 2011).

The ability to communicate and interact with others successfully is vital to ensure success in Key Stage 1 and

Introduction

beyond, which is why communication and language is one of the prime areas in the EYFS.

There is a growing body of research to suggest that technological advances are having a negative impact on the language development of children. Recent research has found that handheld screen time (e.g. playing on phones, tablets and handheld games devices) is linked to delayed language development (ASHA, 2017). Background television has also been found to significantly impact children's attention skills, which play an important role in language development (Schmidt et al, in Spooner and Woodcock, 2010).

Research shows that many children reach the end of the EYFS with delayed skills in communication and language. In areas of deprivation, up to 50% of children are behind in reaching developmental milestones in the area of communication and language when they start school (The Communication Trust, 2011). This highlights the importance of promoting the communication and language development of all children in the early years.

Personal experience has shown that from time to time, practitioners will report that they are unsure whether an EAL learner is picking up English in the typical way, particularly in localities that do not have high numbers of EAL learners. Due to a lack of clear guidance, it can be difficult for practitioners to identify when an EAL learner has additional needs in the prime area of communication and language. For this reason, typical additional language acquisition is discussed to help practitioners identify whether the EAL learners in their setting are following the usual patterns of language acquisition.

No two EAL learners are the same, in fact far from it. If you take two EAL learners, they will most probably have been exposed to different languages and different cultures. They will have different personalities and varying levels of confidence and self-esteem, and their exposure to English and to early years settings may well also differ. This is to mention just a few of the many factors that vary from one child to the next. Due to the diverse nature of EAL learners, practitioners are often left with questions and concerns as how best to support them. This book aims to address such questions.

Introduction

About this book

The main purpose of this book is to give clear guidance to practitioners about how to support the communication and language development of children learning English as an additional language (EAL) in early years settings, with reference to the new 2017 EYFS statutory framework. The book aims to help practitioners and students to feel more confident in their knowledge and ability to support children who are new to English. *English as an additional language (EAL) in practice* is a user-friendly, practical resource that can be referred to when questions or queries arise with an EAL learner in an early years setting.

As well as providing essential information about EAL learners, the book covers several main topics including: how children learn languages, how to prepare for a new starter who has limited or no English, helping children to settle-in, creating a suitable environment, working with parents and observation and assessment. There are also chapters which focus specifically on supporting the prime area of communication and language. Features of typical acquisition of an additional language are explored as well as information about how to identify and support EAL learners who have additional needs in relation to communication and language. The roles and responsibilities of a key person are also discussed in each chapter, in relation to EAL learners.

Parents' views and perspectives are included throughout the book, which provides an interesting insight into many of the key topics. Similarly, reflective comments made by practitioners from a range of different EYFS settings are also included in each section. The practitioner perspective boxes contain some fantastic tips about approaches that have worked in practice in their real life settings. Reflective practice is key to providing great EYFS provision, therefore these reflection boxes are there to support you. Case studies are also included in each chapter to highlight real life situations and occurrences as well as to share examples of good practice.

There is also a resources section at the back of the book containing a range of materials that can be used to support the EAL learners in your setting. This includes vocabulary lists in some of the most common languages spoken in the UK, as well as a selection of home activity sheets to give to parents.

The national picture

'Britain today is culturally and linguistically diverse.'
(Washbourne, 2011)

National statistics show that there is now a greater level of diversity in the UK than there has been in the past. Every ten years, the census is carried out in the UK. The census is an official survey of the members of the population. It gathers information about languages spoken and English proficiency, as well as information on age, gender, health, economic activity, household make up and so on.

The most recent census, carried out in 2011, showed the following:

- Just over 6% of people in the UK spoke a main language that was not English. This equated to over 3,800,000 people.

- The percentage of people who reported speaking a main language other than English had increased since the previous census in 2001.

- Of the people who reported a main language that was not English, the majority could also speak English.

- Just under 1% (0.72%) of people in the UK were unable to speak English, which equated to over 170,000 people.

Note: these figures are based on all usual residents aged 3 years and over at the time of the census.
(Census data gathered from ons.gov.uk, scotlandcensus.gov.uk, nisra.gov.uk)

Regional differences

We know that around 6% of the UK population speak a main language that is not English, however we also know that this 6% of people is not evenly spread across the UK. There are great differences in the distribution of people who speak languages other than English in different areas.

In general, built up urban areas such as cities and larger towns have a higher percentage of people who speak

Introduction

a main language that is not English compared to more rural areas. In small towns and villages, it is much less common for there to be a high percentage of people who speak a main language that is not English.

Below is some information, taken from the 2011 England and Wales census, about the spread and whereabouts of people who reported that English was not their main language:

- In London, 22% of people reported speaking a main language that was not English. This percentage is more than three times larger than any other place in the UK.

- The area with the second highest percentage of people who reported a main language that was not English was the West Midlands, with a figure of 7%.

- In Wales and parts of England, particularly the North East, only a very small percentage of people reported speaking a main language other than English.

Below are the two most contrasting areas in England, in terms of the percentages of people who reported speaking a main language other than English:

- In the London Borough of Newham, over 41% of people reported a main language that was not English.
- In the Local Authority of Redcar and Cleveland in North Yorkshire, 0.7% of people reported main language other than English.

(Census data gathered from ons.gov.uk)

Most reported languages spoken

The 2011 census data showed that nearly 300 languages were spoken by children attending UK schools (Census data, 2011). Although there is no figure for the number of languages spoken in early years settings, the figure is likely to be comparable.

You may have come across a number of families that speak other languages in your work as an early years practitioner. Can you think of some of the languages spoken by some of the families that you have worked with?

Below is data taken from the 2011 census about the most commonly reported languages spoken in England and Wales:
- After English (and Welsh), the second most reported language spoken was Polish
- The third most reported language spoken was Panjabi
- The fourth most reported language spoken was Urdu

Most commonly spoken languages in England and Wales

The table below shows the 20 most commonly spoken languages in England and Wales, taken from the 2011 Census data:

	Language	Percentage of people		Language	Percentage of people
1	English (English or Welsh if in Wales)	92.3%	11	Spanish	0.2%
2	Polish	1%	12	Tamil	0.2%
3	Panjabi	0.5%	13	Turkish	0.2%
4	Urdu	0.5%	14	Italian	0.2%
5	Bengali (with Sylheti and Chatgaya)	0.4%	15	Somali	0.2%
6	Gujarati	0.4%	16	Lithuanian	0.2%
7	Arabic	0.3%	17	German	0.1%
8	French	0.3%	18	Persian/Farsi	0.1%
9	All other Chinese	0.3%	19	Tagalog/Filipino	0.1%
10	Portuguese	0.2%	20	Romanian	0.1%

*All other Chinese excludes mandarin Chinese and Cantonese Chinese
(Office for National Statistics)

Introduction

- The fifth most reported language spoken was Bengali (ons.gov.uk). In Scotland and Northern Ireland, Polish also accounted for 1% of the population in each country, being the most prevalent language after English (and Scots in Scotland).

In the resources section at the back of the book, there is key vocabulary (e.g. hello, goodbye, thank you, yes, no) in some of the most commonly reported languages in England and Wales. This will be a valuable reference tool when you have any new children in your setting who are exposed to any of these languages at home.

What does this mean for EYFS settings?

The census data suggests that, overall, there continues to be an increase in numbers of EAL learners in early years settings. However, when thinking about the numbers of children learning English as an addition language (EAL), this varies tremendously depending on the type of area and region of the UK. Many rural areas see very few EAL children, whereas many cities and large towns are often catering for high number of children learning EAL within their early years settings.

The quotes below from practitioners working in different areas of the UK demonstrate the variety in numbers of EAL children in settings across the country.

"In my ten years here, we've only ever had two or three children who could speak another language"
(Practitioner from a nursery in small town in South Staffordshire)

"About half of the children in the nursery speak a different language at home"
(Practitioner from a nursery in Greater London)

There is also a great amount of variation between settings in terms of the numbers of children that they cater for; some are very small, catering for just a couple of children, others are very large catering for a high number of children. These larger settings are inevitably more likely to see more EAL learners than the very small settings.

Introduction

The EYFS Statutory Framework

All early years settings, regardless of type or size, must meet the requirements set out in the EYFS statutory framework. The framework sets the 'standards for learning, development and care for children from birth to five' (EYFS, 2017) and is available online for settings to download at: www.gov.uk/government/publications/early-years-foundation-stage-framework--2

Requirements for supporting EAL children

There are a number of requirements stated in the statutory framework that relate specifically to learners of English as an additional language. This is to ensure 'equality of opportunity and anti-discriminatory practice, ensuring that every child is included and supported.' (EYFS, 2017)

These requirements are broken down into five separate points.

They will be referred to as the 'EAL requirements' for the purpose of this book, and each one will be discussed at a more practical level within the main chapters. This is so that you feel confident in ensuring that you can meet these requirement for the EAL learners in your setting.

The EAL requirements

EAL requirement 1: Provide opportunities for children to develop and use their home language in play and learning *(Discussed at a practical level in Chapter five)*.

EAL requirement 2: Support their language development at home *(Discussed at a practical level in Chapter six)*.

EAL requirement 3: Ensure that children have sufficient opportunities to learn and reach a good standard in English *(Discussed at a practical level in Chapter five)*.

EAL requirement 4: Assess children's skills in English *(Discussed at a practical level in Chapter seven)*.

EAL requirement 5: If the child does not have a strong grasp of English language, practitioners must explore the child's skills in the home language to establish whether there is cause for concern about language delay *(Discussed at a practical level in Chapter eight)*.

What does the EYFS say?

- 'For children whose home language is not English, providers must take reasonable steps to provide opportunities for children to develop and use their home language in play and learning, supporting their language development at home.'

- 'Providers must also ensure that children have sufficient opportunities to learn and reach a good standard in English language during the EYFS: ensuring children are ready to benefit from the opportunities available to them when they begin Year 1.'

- 'When assessing communication, language and literacy skills, practitioners must assess children's skills in English.'

- 'If a child does not have a strong grasp of English language, practitioners must explore the child's skills in the home language with parents and/or carers, to establish whether there is cause for concern about language delay.' (EYFS, 2017)

The EYFS Overarching Principles

There are four overarching principles that run through the statutory framework document. Excellent practice happens when all practitioners in a setting understand the importance of these principles and use them to underpin their practice. This is because it enables them to support all children as best as possible, regardless of the background of the child. The importance of each of the four principles in relation to EAL children is shown below:

1) '**Every child is a unique child**...' (EYFS, 2017)

Relevance to EAL learners: All children have their own unique personalities, different interests, likes and dislikes as well as different strengths and weaknesses. EAL learners are particularly unique because, as well the differences listed above, they have also been exposed to a different language or languages. They may also have been exposed to a different culture, a different religion, a different household structure,

Introduction

a different experience of early education and much more. In addition, every EAL learner will respond differently when they start in a new language setting. It is essential that assumptions are not made about a child simply based on the language that they speak or the country that they come from. Every single child is completely unique.

2) 'Children learn to be strong and independent through **positive relationships**' (EYFS, 2017)

Relevance to EAL learners: The role of the **key person** and the relationship that this person builds with learners of EAL is of utmost importance. This is because these children may require a high level of emotional support as they are in an unfamiliar language environment.

'In moments of strong emotion – whether we feel very sad, stressed or happy – we all need someone to share our feelings with.' (Soni and Bristow (2012) Young children experience more 'moments of strong emotion' than adults; when in a new language environment they might feel nervous, confused, worried, shy, upset, bored, tired, self-conscious or angry. It is likely that they will feel a combination of these emotions, so they need someone they can go to for comfort, help or reassurance.

3) 'Children learn and develop well in **enabling environments**' (EYFS, 2017)

Relevance to EAL learners: An early years setting can be a very daunting place for a child who is not familiar with the main language spoken there. There are changes that can be made to the environment that will make it easier for EAL learners to settle-in and feel more relaxed and comfortable, which is essential for children to learn and develop in the setting. For example, introducing a visual timetable can help to make the setting more predictable for EAL learners.

Ensuring that there are resources and materials that reflect the backgrounds and cultures of all children is also key.

4) '**Children develop and learn in different ways and at different rates**' (EYFS, 2017)

Relevance to EAL learners: Regardless of whether they are exposed to one language or several, there will be some children in your setting who are exceeding in the areas of learning and development and other children who are at a level that would be typical for a child of a younger age.

EAL learners are very likely to have different abilities in each of the languages that they are exposed to. As a result, they may respond differently when spoken to in English compared to when spoken to in a more dominant language. Some children go through a silent period when exposed to a new language in an early years setting. This period can last just a matter of days or weeks, or it can continue for many months. Some children do not even enter a silent period at all.

It is also important to be aware that all children develop at different rates in all areas of development and learning and the way in which children learn best may be impacted by previous experiences. For example, a child may not naturally take opportunities to learn through play when they first enter the setting if they have come from a culture that does not encourage play.

Introduction

Settings used for case studies

The author has worked closely with three nurseries in different parts of the UK to gather a range of case studies and to share examples of good practice. These nurseries are located in the following places: Greater London, Stoke-on-Trent, Newcastle upon Tyne.

Early Years Setting 1
Location: Greater London
Type of setting: school nursery

There are 82 children on roll at the setting.
Over 50% of the children on roll are EAL learners.

After English, the most commonly spoken languages in this setting are Somali, Panjabi, Bengali, Polish.

Early Years Setting 2
Location: Stoke-on-Trent
Type of setting: school nursery

There are 30 children on roll at the setting.
20% of children on roll are EAL learners.

After English, the most commonly spoken languages in this setting are: Urdu, Polish, Panjabi, Romanian.

Early Years Setting 3
Location: Newcastle upon Tyne
Type of setting: school nursery

There are 50 children on roll at the setting.
2% of children are EAL learners (1 child).

The language spoken by the EAL learner in the setting is Polish.

Throughout the book, these three early years settings will be referred to, as they have all been recognised for their good practice in terms of inclusion and some more specifically for their ability to support EAL children. Examples of good practice from each setting as well as staff perspectives and tips are featured throughout the book.

Brief outline of each chapter

Chapter One: EAL Essentials
This chapter discusses what is meant by the term EAL and explores different groups of EAL learners (simultaneous learners and sequential learners). It also defines other terms including 'bilingualism' and 'new arrival'. Key facts about EAL learners are explored; a good starting point for all, particularly those who are new to supporting EAL learners. Reading this chapter should enable you to feel more confident in your overall knowledge about EAL learners.

Chapter Two: How children learn languages
This chapter explores how children learn their first language before highlighting the steps that children usually go through when they are exposed to a new language. Factors that can impact additional language learning are discussed, including the child's ability in their first language, the environment and the child's communication style and overall well-being. Chapter two also explains how children who are exposed to two languages from birth (or shortly after) learn two languages at the same time.

Chapter Three: Helping children to settle-in
The chapter is split into three parts:
   a) Before the child starts
   b) The child's first day
   c) The child's first few weeks.

Each of the three parts offer a wealth of advice and practical ideas about helping children settle-in to your early years setting, with a selection of insightful perspectives from parents and practitioners.

Chapter Four: Creating a suitable environment
Chapter four focuses on how to create a suitable environment to support the children in the setting who are new to the English language. The principles of 'Communication Friendly Settings' outlined by Elizabeth Jarman (2006) are explored, including changes to the layout of the room, the materials available, the displays and much more. Environmental changes that can help make children and their families feel welcomed and valued are also discussed.

Introduction

Chapter Five: Adult-child interaction
This chapter offers advice and strategies about how best to interact with children to support them to learn English. It looks at how to interact with babies and toddlers who are learning two languages at the same time, as well as children who are learning English after developing skills in their first language. The focus at the end of the chapter is on play as this is such a powerful tool for language learning in the early years.

Chapter Six: Building positive relationships with parents and carers
This chapter explores how best to work with parents to develop strong and positive relationships. It raises potential challenges that you might face and provides a wealth of suggestions about how to overcome these challenges. The chapter also explores how to make best use of interpreters. Parents' viewpoints give a crucial insight into some of the topics raised in this chapter.

Chapter Seven: Assessment, observation and planning
Chapter seven focuses on the observation, assessment and planning cycle and gives practical advice about how to meet the requirements set out in the EYFS statutory framework when working with EAL learners. It also discusses how to complete a summative assessment for the EAL learners in your setting for the 2 year check as well as at the end of EYFS.

Chapter Eight: Working with children with communication difficulties
This chapter is split into three parts:
a) Understanding Speech, Language and Communication Needs (SLCN)
b) Identifying SLCN in EAL learners
c) Supporting EAL learners with SLCN.

As well as exploring how to identify children with additional language and communication difficulties amongst children learning EAL, this chapter also looks at how to support any EAL learners who have communication and language needs.

Resources section
Here you will find a wealth of practical resources for your setting, including a range of home activity sheets, an 'all about me' template and a pre-start parent meeting checklist. There are also lists of essential vocabulary in some of the most commonly spoken languages in the UK.

Chapter One
EAL Essentials

With over 300 languages being spoken in the UK (Literacy Trust, 2000), more and more early years settings are now catering for children who speak languages other than English. It is therefore essential that practitioners have good background knowledge of terminology as well as vital matters that are true of all EAL learners. This chapter explains the terms EAL and bilingualism and identifies the different groups of EAL learners. It then explores the following four 'key EAL matters':

1) The importance of the home language
2) The existence of cultural differences
3) The emotional impact of being in a new language environment
4) The possibility of a silent period.

This chapter is a great starting point for anyone who is relatively new to supporting EAL children as it provides essential information that will inform your practice. An awareness of these key matters will greatly enhance your understanding of the EAL learners and hence guide your sensitive approach and all-important interaction.

What does EAL mean?

EAL refers to children who are **learning English as an additional language**.

'The government definition of an EAL learner includes anyone who has been exposed to a language other than English during early childhood and continues to be exposed to this language in the home or in the community.' (eal.britishcouncil.org)

The term EAL is used to describe 'a diverse group of pupils for whom English is an additional language.

Chapter One EAL Essentials

What they have in common is that they use one or more language other than English at home or in their community.' (eal.britishcouncil.org)

Note: In books and resources relating to EAL learners, you may see the terms 'home language', 'first language', 'mother tongue' and 'preferred language' used to refer to the other language that a child hears and uses at home. This book will use the terms 'first language' and 'home language' interchangeably.

Groups of EAL learners

Children learning English as an additional language are an incredibly diverse group of individuals, however they typically fit into one of the two groups outlined below:

Simultaneous learners

Some children are **exposed to more than one language as a baby or toddler**. Those introduced to more than one language before the age of 3 are typically classed as simultaneous learners, as they are learning two (or more) languages at the same time (Auer & Wei, 2007).

For example, a child with a Polish mother and an English father who is spoken to in Polish and English from birth would fall into this group. Similarly, a toddler spoken to only in Albanian until the child started a private nursery in the UK at 16 months old would also be classed as a simultaneous learner.

Case Study: Fatma

Age: 3 years old

Fatma was born in Greater London. Her mother is from Turkey and her father is from the UK.

Fatma's parents have spoken to her in both Turkish and English since she was born.

She also has two older siblings who speak English to one another much of the time at home.

Fatma is a simultaneous learner of Turkish and English.

Sequential learners

Other children begin **learning English after learning their first language**. Sequential acquisition occurs when 'another language is introduced after the child has a sound command of the first language.' (Soni, 2013) A child is usually classed as a sequential learner when exposed to a new language after reaching the age of 3 years (Auer & Wei, 2007).

This often occurs when a child's family moves to the UK from another country, or if parents speak a language other than English at home and then the child starts at an early years setting.

Many children who fall into this group are exposed to English for the first time when they start nursery or reception.

Case Study: Grzegorz

Age: 3 years, 3 months

Grzegorz has lived in the UK since birth but has only been spoken to in Polish at home.

Both parents are originally from Poland; they moved to the UK when Grzegorz's mother was pregnant with him. Grzegorz doesn't have any siblings.

The family have several friends in the local area, all of whom are also Polish.

Grzegorz has heard small amounts of English when out and about with his parents.

He has recently started nursery where he is being properly exposed to English for the first time.

Grzegorz is a sequential learner. He is learning English after gaining good skills in Polish.

Chapter One EAL Essentials

Case Study: Aisha

Age: 4 years old

Aisha has recently moved to the UK with her family from Somalia. While living in Somalia, Aisha was using Somali and Arabic. She had been exposed to both languages from birth. On arrival in the UK, Aisha started nursery almost immediately, which is where she was first properly submerged into the English language.

From birth, Aisha was simultaneously learning Somali and Arabic.

She is now sequentially learning English.

No two EAL learners are the same

The case studies above begin to highlight differences in terms of languages spoken and exposure to English. Some EAL children in your setting will have had little or no exposure to English before they enter your setting, whereas other EAL learners will already have been exposed to English for a while.

Some EAL children in your setting may have lived in the UK since birth; others may have moved to the UK from another country.

New arrivals

The term new arrival refers to a child who has recently moved to this country and who is being exposed to English, possibly for the first time, as a result of this move.

New arrivals may have moved to the country for one of many reasons, for example:

- They may be economic migrants who have moved to seek employment or in search of better opportunities for their family.

- They may have left their home country to escape war or other dangers and therefore are seeking asylum in the UK.

The British Council highlight that, 'as well as differences in the language levels and use of language of the various groups of EAL learners, there is also huge variation in terms of a range of other factors.' (eal.britishcouncil.org) These factors include: social class and economic status, educational background, religion, political affiliation, cultural background, ethnicity, literacy, ability, knowledge and experience of the UK.

EAL learners have experienced a vast range of different personal circumstances and so they have a wide variety of individual needs. It is very important to work closely with parents to share information about all aspects of a child's situation and development to ensure that all children are supported appropriately. There are many ideas about information sharing and partnership working with parents in Chapters three and six.

What is bilingualism?

Put simply, bilingualism refers to the ability to use more than one language. However there are actually many different definitions of bilingualism. Franson (2011) explains that 'to be bilingual means different things to different people.'

English as an additional language (EAL) in practice

Chapter One EAL Essentials

Some definitions state that a person must reach a certain skill level in two languages in order to be classed as bilingual. A number of older definitions also state that a person must have equal abilities in each language to be referred to as bilingual.

Many of the more recent definitions describe a person as bilingual regardless of their level of ability in each language with the recognition that the use of each language will vary, therefore it is not realistic to expect an equally high level of language skills in each language.

The definition below, written by Madhani (1994) does not specify how competent an individual must be in either language to be referred to as bilingual. He states that individuals are bilingual if they '…understand and use two or more languages to varying degrees and at various times.' (Madhani, 1994 cited in Buckley, 2003)

This definition refers to people who are not necessarily equally fluent or literate in both languages, but who have access to, or need to use two or more languages at home and at school or work for example.

Soni (2013) highlights the difficulties with defining the term bilingualism and states that 'the unique way people acquire and use language makes it difficult to define bilingualism accurately. It is a subjective and personal view.' (Soni, 2013)

For individuals who use more than one language, each language serves different purposes and is used in different places and with different people. So bilingualism is not just about proficiency, it is also about use and experience.

In relation to children, the term 'bilingual learner' applies to 'all pupils who use or have access to more than one language at home or at school – it does not necessarily imply full fluency in both or all languages.' (DfE 2003)' (eal.britishcouncil.org) Many education staff therefore use the term 'bilingual pupils' rather than 'learner of EAL' in their setting, or they may use the terms interchangeably.

Chapter One EAL Essentials

Key EAL matters

This next section outlines four key matters to be aware of in relation to EAL learners.

1) The importance of the home language
2) The existence of cultural differences
3) The emotional impact of being in a new language environment
4) The possibility of a silent period.

These factors will all be explored in some detail below, with examples and case studies as well as practitioner and parent perspectives. It is important that anyone who is supporting children learning English as an additional language is aware of these four key EAL matters.

Key EAL matter 1: The child's home language is of great importance

There is a wealth of research that shows how important a child's first language is for their ongoing development in all areas. Gibbons (1991) and Soni (2013) both explain why a child's first language is so important and why children should continue to develop and use their home language, as well as highlighting what might happen if children are not given opportunities to use and develop their home language.

Why is the first language so important?

- The first language plays a vital role in learning new things and trying to make sense of new concepts. Using the child's home language for learning allows the child to 'draw on their total language experience and so continue their conceptual development' (Gibbons, 1991). Children who have weaker skills in their first language have 'fewer pegs on which to hang new learning' (Gibbons, 1991).

- The first language also plays an important role in the acquisition of additional languages. EAL learners who are new to your setting 'with a strong command of their first language and a developed range of concepts in that language are thus in a very favourable position to learn English.' (Gibbons, 1991)

Continuing to develop skills in the home language makes it easier for a child to develop skills in English as an additional language. 'Developing and maintaining a home language as the foundation for knowledge about language will support the development of English and should be encouraged.' (Department for Children, Schools and Families, 2007)

What happens if the child has limited exposure to the home language?

- If a child's home language is not encouraged at home or at school or nursery, this can bring about delayed skills in other areas of the child's development, as the home language is vital for learning and development.

- They are likely to find it difficult to learn new concepts and understand new things if exposure to their home language stops and they do not have the opportunity to discuss and talk about new concepts in their home language.

- It can also lead to 'subtractive bilingualism', which is where the child loses the skills that they had

English as an additional language (EAL) in practice

Chapter One EAL Essentials

developed in their home language, with English becoming the predominant language. (Soni, 2013) As a result, children can lose the ability to communicate with family members such as grandparents.

- If exposure to the first language stops, children can experience difficulties with their own sense of identity, and feel confusion about who they are as a person (Franson, 2011). This can impact their personal, social and emotional development.

- Sometimes parents think that it will help their child if they start speaking English all the time at home, rather than using their home language. If a parent tries to speak a language that they are not so good at, this will make it hard for the child to make progress with their own language development as they will not be hearing good language models.

Parents should continue to speak their own language at home. It is far better for the child if parents speak the language(s) that they are best at and most comfortable with. This way, children are hearing a good language model.

As well as hearing and using their first language at home, children also need opportunities to do this when in their early years setting. For the reasons above, it is vital to 'balance a child's need to learn English with their right to maintain their first or home language.' (Soni, 2013)

Throughout this book there are tips and ideas about how best to ensure that children have the opportunity to develop their skills in their home language both at home and whilst in your setting.

Key EAL matter 2: It is essential to be aware of cultural differences

'Learning a language and becoming bilingual is also about learning and living in different societies and cultures. It is not just about acquiring a new language, but also about **understanding another culture** and developing another identity.' (Franson, 2011)

As well as hearing and using different languages, EAL learners may have been exposed to a different culture. From culture to culture, there are differences in the way people act and behave, as well as differences in views and attitudes towards various things. An action or behaviour may be thought of as rude or even unacceptable in one culture, yet considered to be perfectly acceptable and part of everyday life in another culture.

The term 'culture shock' is sometimes used to refer to the experience of being in a culture that in incredibly different to what we are used to in many ways. This term emphasises the great degree to which cultures can vary.

> ### Reflection
>
> Can you think of any cultural differences that you have experienced for yourself? For example, have you ever been to another country where it is not the norm to queue? If so, how did you feel in this situation? This is an example of how some cultures differ to our UK culture.

You may notice differences in the way some EAL learners behave, some of which could be down to cultural norms. You may also notice cultural differences in the behaviours

Chapter One EAL Essentials

and views of the parents of some of the EAL children in your setting. Of course, all people differ and we can't make assumptions about people or generalise. However, having an awareness of some cultural differences can help you to understand some behaviours that you might see in children or parents. Similarly it might explain the reason for some comments that parents might make. It will also help you to better understand how to approach children in certain situations. Having an awareness of cultural differences may potentially avoid misunderstandings or misinterpretations.

Examples of cultural differences

- **Non-verbal communication**
  There are different norms when it comes to body language and other forms of non-verbal communication, such as gestures and eye contact. For example, some children will avoid eye contact as looking directly at teachers is considered to be disrespectful in some cultures. It is useful to be aware that 'East Asian students often close their eyes when concentrating' (tefl.net), which can often be misinterpreted. In some cultures, crossing one leg other the other when sitting on a chair is considered rude. In some cultures women do not shake hands.

- **Play**
  There are differences in attitudes towards play across cultures. In some cultures, adults don't typically play with children. Here in the UK we are highly passionate about play and the benefits of play. Cultural differences in play are explored more on pages 62-63.

- **Dress/clothing**
  Views on what is considered to be appropriate attire can vary from one culture to another. Some cultures consider it to be inappropriate or rude for women to show their shoulders or legs, particularly their thighs and knees. Some women cover their hair with a veil called a hijab for religious reasons.

- **Food and drink**
  You can probably think of differences in the types of foods and drinks that are typically consumed in some cultures and you may be able to think of examples of food from different countries. There are also differences in the way people from different cultures behave at mealtimes. For example, in some cultures it is polite to leave a small amount of food on your plate because to clear your plate implies that you were not given enough food and that you are not satisfied. In other cultures, it is considered to be incredibly rude and disrespectful to leave any food on your plate.

  It is important to also be aware of religious practices, such as Ramadan which is a period of fasting during daylight hours observed by Muslims.

- **Attitudes towards making mistakes and getting things wrong**
  In some cultures, children will avoid answering a question unless they are absolutely certain that they know the correct answer. In many non-western cultures, getting an answer wrong was linked to punishment in the past and in some cultures it still is today. Getting things wrong therefore can cause learners from some cultures to feel great embarrassment and humiliation. For this reason, people from some cultures can also be very reluctant to admit that they don't understand something or ask for help or clarification. It is important to be aware of this if supporting learners from non-western cultures, particularly if they have recently moved from their home country.

- **Gender roles**
  There are differences in views of the typical role that men and women take in a family in some cultures. British customs are typically relatively relaxed when it comes to gender roles in comparison to some cultures, who consider women to take on a less important role than men. As part of attitudes towards gender roles, expectations of roles and completion of household chores and tasks vary. Similarly, very high expectations can be placed on boys in comparison to girls in some cultures. Attitudes towards the types of toys that boys and girls are exposed to can also vary.

- **Topics that are considered to be taboo**
  In some cultures, it is not commonplace to discuss certain topics including: money, pregnancy, female family members, dogs, the police, politics, social classes, certain periods of history, race, sexual orientation. (www.tefl.net, 2017) In addition, many people are patriotic and very proud of their background and enjoy talking about their home country. However some people, for example some asylum seekers or refugees would rather not share information about the country that they are from and their status in the UK.

Chapter One EAL Essentials

- **Conversational norms**
  Cultural differences exist in relation to making small talk, silence during conversations, directness when talking, and interrupting.

- **Attitudes towards special educational needs and disabilities (SEND)**
  In some cultures, people are not as accepting of disabilities and special educational needs. Some cultures believe that for example, a child has been 'cursed' or will bring bad luck to the future of their family if a child has a disability or an additional need.

The list of cultural differences goes on. This is just a quick overview of some of the main differences that you are likely to come across when working with EAL learners.

Some EAL learners who have recently started an early years setting will be unfamiliar with many of the cultural customs in the UK. As well as attempting to understand the new language that they are now exposed to, they will have to make sense of some of the behaviours and expectations of the people in the setting.

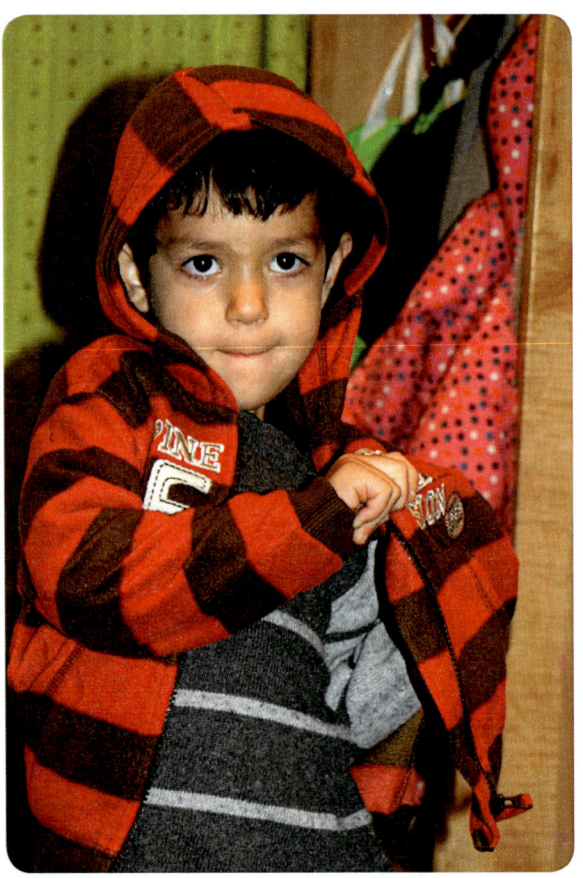

Case Study: cultural differences

Child's name: Chi Yat
Age: 5 years old

Chi Yat is a new arrival who previously lived in Japan. Every morning he bows to his teacher and teaching assistant when he enters the classroom. His teachers have also noticed the following: he does not make eye contact, he will answer questions when he is sure of the answer but he will not have a guess.

After a conversation with the school's EAL coordinator, his teacher now has a much better understanding of the cultural customs of Japan. She is now aware of the following:

- It is seen as disrespectful to make sustained eye contact
- Bowing to elders/people in a higher status position is a sign of respect
- Getting things wrong can be the cause of humiliation and embarrassment, therefore 'saving face' and avoiding humiliation is considered to be very important.

Key EAL matter 3: EAL learners are likely to experience a range of emotions

Being in an environment where you understand very little of what is being said around you is not an easy experience. Children may feel anxious, worried, confused or upset, to name just a few of the common emotions often felt by young children who are in an unfamiliar language environment.

Put yourself in the shoes of a young child who does not understand the language spoken in their new nursery. Think about how you might feel in this situation. You may feel isolated, helpless, unsure of yourself and lonely.

For a new EAL learner, the people in their setting may look and sound different to those in their home environment. People may speak in a different language, act in new ways, and demand new ways of behaving and responding. It may take a child a while to know what is expected of them and to trust unfamiliar adults.

Chapter One EAL Essentials

'It is important to look out for any signs of stress, anxiety and aggression that may exhibit themselves in this unfamiliar context.' (Sood and Mistry, 2015)

As well as causing a child to experience many of the emotions mentioned above, being in an early years setting is thought to be much more tiring for EAL learners than for children whose first language is English. This is because many EAL learners are continually doing each of the following:

- Trying to understand the new language
- Trying to understand the expectations of the setting
- Getting used to cultural differences.

All of these things require a high level of mental effort. Similarly experiencing high levels of emotions such as anxiety for periods of time can also be incredibly tiring in itself.

In Chapter three this key EAL matter is explored in more detail in relation to the role of the key person in supporting EAL learners during this potentially emotionally challenging time.

Reflection

Have you ever been in a country where you do not speak the language?
Have you ever been given a menu written in a language that you don't understand?
Have you had to try and ask for directions?
Was this an easy task? How did you feel at the time?

Key EAL matter 4: Many EAL learners go through a silent period

Many children go through a silent period when they are exposed to a new language environment. This is a very typical part of learning a new language that can last from a couple of weeks to several months. During this period, children are listening and taking in their new language.

There is more information about the silent period in Chapters three and five. If you have any children in your setting who are current going through this phase, there is advice about how to support children during this period on page 59.

Chapter Two How children learn languages

The way children learn to understand and use language is a fascinating process. In just a few short years, many parents go from eagerly anticipating their child's first words to wondering when they'll next get peace and quiet. This chapter explores how children learn languages, firstly by looking at first language acquisition and outlining key developmental milestones.

Routes to bilingualism are then explored. The chapter outlines how children who are exposed to more than one language simultaneously as a baby or young toddler learn these languages.

It then looks as sequential learners, highlighting steps that children usually go through when exposed to a new language after learning a first. Factors that can impact on additional language learning are discussed.

The term **receptive language skills** refers to a child's ability to understand the words that they hear and to understand the meaning of what people are saying to them.

> 'Receptive language is indeed at the heart of all other aspects of learning language, whether is it your first language or a subsequent language acquisition. It is essential that a child is able to recognise sounds and differentiate words, to follow instructions, and to learn sentences, rhymes and songs.' (Hayes, 2016)

The term **expressive language skills** refers to a child's ability to use words to communicate. Being able to name people, objects and actions as well as making requests and asking questions all require expressive language. Developing expressive language skills is more complex than simply learning words. Children need to learn how to put words together which requires them to learn the rules of the language.

Chapter Two How children learn languages

First language acquisition

During their first days and weeks of life, babies begin to 'tune-in' to the voices of their main carers and distinguish between different voice tones, such as soothing sounds, singing and more playful conversation sounds. There is an incredible rate of development in all areas during the early years, and receptive language development is a major area of growth. Within the first year, babies will start to develop an understanding of the meaning of a number of words that they hear regularly in meaningful situations.

As well as developing an awareness of the noises and sounds that their main carers are making, babies soon begin to experiment with their own voice as they coo and babble. Many babies attempt to say their first word somewhere between 10 and 15 months old. They will continue to develop skills in both receptive language (understanding language) and expressive language (using words) throughout their childhood. Children usually understand far more than they can say, as most children's receptive language skills are ahead of their expressive language skills.

What does the EYFS say?

By the end of the EYFS, it is expected that children are able to do the following:

Understanding: 'children follow instructions involving several ideas or actions. They answer 'how' and 'why' questions about their experiences and in response to stories and events.' (EYFS, 2017)

Speaking: 'children express themselves effectively, showing awareness of listeners' needs. They use past, present and future forms accurately when talking about events that have happened or are to happen in the future. They develop their own narratives and explanations by connecting ideas or events.' (EYFS, 2017)

There are of course many steps and milestones that children must reach in order to achieve these early learning goals. These will be explored next.

Chapter Two How children learn languages

The table below looks at the receptive language skills (understanding) and the expressive language skills (talking) of children from birth to the end of the EYFS age range.

The information in the table applies to children who are exposed to just one language from birth; these milestones are based on children learning English as a mother tongue.

First Language Acquisition Developmental Milestones

Age	Receptive language skills (understanding)	Expressive language skills (talking)
By 6 months	During the first six months of life, babies tune in and listen to the sounds that they hear. They may have some understanding of words such as 'no', 'bye bye', 'all gone' and 'more' when these words are accompanied with gesture and used in context.	They typically make a range of different noises and experiment with their voices through babbling and other sounds.
By 12-18 months	By this point, toddlers typically show some understanding of words that refer to familiar items and familiar people (e.g. mummy, daddy, teddy, car, dog, juice). They are able to point to a range of people and items when asked (e.g. 'where's teddy?').	Most children say their first words at around 12 months. Of course, it may be a little before or after this age. First they tend to learn the words for familiar items, familiar people and social words (e.g. daddy, juice, bye). Verbs (e.g. jump, sleep, eat) come a little later than nouns.
By 18 months-2 years	Children are usually able to follow simple instructions, when they choose to of course. They can typically follow instructions that contain 1-2 key words (e.g. 'where's daddy?' or 'where's the big teddy?').	Toddlers typically start to join words at around this stage. For example, they might say phrases such as: 'no mummy', 'daddy gone', 'more juice', 'juice all gone'.
By 2-3 years	Children typically understand instructions that contain 2–3 key words (e.g. 'where's the big red ball?')	Children typically attempt to make longer utterances by this point, however they can continue to struggle to get their message across to others at times and will rely on non-verbal communication when necessary.
By 3-4 years	Children are able to understand more lengthy instructions and can understand some 'wh' questions such as 'who' questions and 'where' questions. Their understanding of prepositions (e.g. in, on, under, behind) will typically have developed or will be developing.	Expressive language skills are much more advanced by this stage, however children will continue to generalise grammatical rules resulting in errors such as '…two mouses' and 'I goed to the park'.
By 4-5 years	Children are typically able to follow a string of 2-3 instructions. They will have a good understanding of a wider range of linguistic concepts including: sequences (first, next), textures (smooth, rough), characteristics (old, new), emotional states (happy, sad, scared), quantities (many, few, some), spatial relationships (top, bottom, behind, above).	By the end of the EYFS, children are typically able to engage in conversations with adults. They are able to explain something that has happened and talk in the past and future tense. They will typically ask familiar people a high number of questions.
(Adapted from the following sources: Bowen, 1998; Sheridan, 2008)		

Chapter Two How children learn languages

Children following this common progress in their communication and language development are likely to meet the expected requirements (the early learning goals) by the end of the EYFS.

How does first language acquisition vary between languages?

Languages vary in many ways. As well as having different vocabularies, languages vary in terms of the sounds used in the language, the sentence structures and the grammatical rules. Therefore there may be some differences in the stages of language acquisition for children learning a language other than English.

Babies of all languages experiment with their voices within the first weeks and months of life, however the sounds they use in vocal play and babbling actually reflect the sounds of the language(s) they hear. For example, babies who are spoken to in French will use different sounds in their babble to babies who have been exposed to English. (Maguire-Fong, 2015)

Similarly, by around 12 months, children tend to begin to say their first attempts at words regardless of language. However, some difference in the expressive language milestones can be seen from this point onwards, due to differences between languages. For example, in English, children tend to start naming nouns before they use verbs; however this is not true of all language. In Korean for example, children tend to learn verbs before nouns. (Tomasello, 2014)

In general though, regardless of the language they are exposed to, typical language acquisition follows the main developmental milestones shown in the table on page 22, with the usual variation from child to child.

Learning two languages simultaneously

In many ways, the stages that simultaneous language learners go through mirror the way monolingual children learn language. Babies exposed to two or more languages will coo and babble in the same way as monolingual children, however they may use a wider range of sounds when babbling, reflecting the languages that they hear (Maguire-Fong, 2015).

They will then start to use single words in one or both languages at around the 12 month stage, before then joining words in the months that follow. The amount of exposure that each child has to each language will vary, as will many other factors, such as the quality of the language models that they are hearing, therefore it is almost inevitable that children have different abilities in each of their languages. Typically though, children will understand more than they can say in each language that they are exposed to.

A child's early vocabulary in each language is often smaller than a monolingual child's vocabulary. However when the number of words that they know in both languages are combined, the figure is usually much the same as a monolingual child's vocabulary (Cote and Bornstein, 2015). Simultaneous learners develop two separate but connected language systems. They will at some point notice that there are two words for the same thing and develop an awareness of the two languages.

Chapter Two How children learn languages

As well as being exposed to more than one vocabulary, simultaneous language learners are also exposed to 'a more diverse set of linguistic structures than monolingual children.' (MacLeod, et al, 2013) In attempts to express themselves, it is common that these children attempt to apply the rules of one language to the other language. Similarly, when they speak, it is typical for them to continue to use words from both languages within one sentence. This is referred to as code switching.

The research shows that, before reaching school age, many sequential language learners 'develop linguistic systems that are comparable to monolingual peers at least in one language or in both languages.' (MacLeod, et al, 2013)

Case Study: Maria

Age: 2 years, 9 months
Languages: Polish and English

Maria was born in the West Midlands in the UK to her Polish parents.

Maria's parents have spoken to her in Polish since she was born and she has been looked after by a childminder from 8am-1pm on weekdays since the age of 5 months. Maria's childminder only speaks English.

Maria said her first words in Polish at 13 months. By 16 months she had started using single words in both Polish and English to request her favourite things, including juice, ball and her favourite soft toys. She then started joining words by 20 months in English.

Maria will now create short phrases, containing 3-4 words in both languages and her childminder and parents are hearing her say new words every single day.

How do children learn an additional language?

This section looks at how sequential learners (aged 3 years and above) go about learning an additional language. Sequential learners are those who are exposed to a new language after gaining some language ability in their first language(s).

The way sequential learners acquire a new language is different to how they learnt their first language. This is because they are able to draw on the knowledge that they already have about how languages work. An EAL learner with no prior experience of English may already understand that '…words refer to objects and events, that words can be combined to form phrases and sentences, and that application of grammatical rules can change the tense of an utterance' (Madhani, 1994 cited in Buckley, 2003). They will use this knowledge to try and figure out which of the rules and patterns from their first language apply to English and which rules and patterns don't apply or work in this new language. This is a strategy that children who are just learning one language are not able to use.

Franson (2011) explains that 'first language knowledge will be helpful in the acquisition of the second language. The extent of this help will be dependent upon their proficiency in their first language, their age and other factors.'

Sequential learners of English will make some of the same errors as monolingual children. For example, they will overgeneralise grammatical rules, such as adding an 's' to all nouns to make them plural (e.g. saying 'mouses' instead of 'mice' and saying 'mans' instead of 'men'). However they will also make other errors that monolingual children wouldn't make, as they attempt to apply a rule from one of their languages to another language.

On average, children take up to two years to become proficient at conversational level in a new language (Murphy, 2011). During this time they have to learn not only new words, but also all of the rules of their new language.

Stages of additional language acquisition

As already discussed, all EAL learners are different. The learning of an additional language varies from child to child, however children who already have good skills in their first language (i.e. sequential learners aged 3+) typically go through many of the stages below when put into a new language environment:

Chapter Two How children learn languages

Stage 1: Attempting to use home language
- Children usually try and use their home language at first.
- They tend to learn relatively quickly that their first language doesn't work in this new setting.
- For the majority of children, this period is typically very brief, lasting up to a week or two. For some children this lasts a little longer, usually no longer than 2-4 months.

Stage 2: Silent period
- Many children go through a silent period after their initial attempts to use their home language, however not all children do.
- This period can last anywhere from a couple of weeks to several months. Younger children may stay silent for longer than slightly older children.
- Be aware that this is by no means a passive period. The children are listening to and taking in their new language all of the time. They are developing their ability to understand their new language.

'All the time these children will be watching and listening and gradually taking in the English language that is being used around them.' (Sargent, 2016)

- They often attempt to communicate using non-verbal communication, such as gestures, pointing and bringing items to adults.
- The more a child interacts with peers during this stage, the more likely they are to start attempting to use words more quickly.
- Be aware that children may be more willing to have a go at using their new language during play with other children and away from the gaze of adults.

It is important that you feel confident in your ability to support children who are at this stage. For more advice about how to support children who are going through a silent period, see page 59.

Stage 3: First attempts to use new language
- When first attempting to use the new language, children will typically use one word utterances (e.g. naming objects).
- They may use some short phrases that they have memorised (e.g. 'I don't know', 'What's happening?').
- They may also repeat or echo words or phrases that they hear. For example, if an adult says 'do you want milk?', the child might reply with 'want milk' or simply 'milk'.
- When they first try to join words themselves, their attempts will typically be telegrammatic. This means that they will only use the most important words, missing out the smaller grammatical words. For example, 'more juice', 'ball gone'.
- They might start to join in with key words or phrases in stories and songs, which they have learnt by listening and copying others.
- You may see a child use the same simple structure when attempting to join words (e.g. 'I want apple', 'I want toilet', 'I want home' or 'I do ball', 'I do toilet').

Stage 4: Improving use of new language
- After stage 3, children typically continue to develop their skills in the new language; however they usually continue to make a high number of mistakes, particularly with their choice of words and their use of grammar.
- EAL learners often make mistakes that are typical of a younger child in the language they are learning, such as missing off the plural 's' and overusing the '-ed' ending.
- They will also make mistakes as a result of trying to apply the rules of their first language to English.

Chapter Two How children learn languages

- They will often overuse very general words such as 'doing' and 'going' (e.g. 'doing the ball' rather than 'throwing the ball').
- They will begin to use basic question words (e.g. where, who).
- They find context based conversations (i.e. talking about what is happening around them in the 'here and now') easier to join in with compared to conversations that are not related to their immediate environment.
- They will begin to use independent phrases, e.g. to express dislikes, etc.
- They will begin to use extended phrases using adjectives as well as nouns and verbs (e.g. 'Look, doggie run fast').
- They will eventually reach the stage of using longer sentences and being able to get their intended message across the majority of the time, although some minor 'irregularities' may still occur as they continue to understand the rules of their new language.
- It can take over 2 years for children to be able to produce grammatical structures accurately and consistently. (dorsetforyou.gov.uk)

Code-Switching

Many children who are exposed to more than one language will mix their home language and the new language within sentences, as their skills in the new language develop. Code-switching is not a sign that the child is confused; it is a completely normal part of language development for children who are learning more than one language. (Elks & McLachlan, 2016)

Case Study: Abdirahim

Child's age: 5 years
Home language: Somali

Abdirahim started nursery at the age of 3 years and 2 months. This was when he was first exposed to English properly. Before then, he had only been exposed to Somali within the family home. When he joined the setting, he had age appropriate skills in Somali and parents reported that he was 'good at talking'.

Abdirahim's key person reported that, despite being completed unfamiliar with English, he settled very well into the nursery. Abdirahim went through a short silent period during his first couple of months at nursery, however during this time he joined in with the other children in the nursery garden most mornings.

After half a term in nursery Abdirahim began using some English words and then his English vocabulary grew quickly. He has now been exposed to English for almost 2 years and although he makes many errors when speaking English, he confidently attempts to use new words and make longer sentences in this language, both at nursery and at home with his younger brother.

Factors that impact on additional language learning

The speed at which EAL learners manage to master skills in the English language varies from child to child, however there are a number of factors that will impact

Chapter Two How children learn languages

the rate and ease at which a child develops skills in an additional language. Here are some reasons for individual differences in acquiring a new language:

- **The amount of exposure to the new language**
  Development in each language depends on exposure and experience. It follows that children who have more exposure to a new language are more likely to learn the new language quicker than children who are not exposed to it as much. So children who are doing full days in early years settings may be in a better position to learn the new language than children who are only in the environment for a couple of hours per day (half days).

- **Environment**
  Chapter four explores ways in which early years settings can be made into excellent environments for EAL learners. The more 'communication friendly' the environment, the better.

- **Adult-child interaction**
  The quality of the adult-child interactions (i.e. the way the adults interact with the child) hugely impacts the child's ability to learn a new language. In Chapter five, there are a range of tips about how best to interact with children who are new to the English language.

- **The child's communication style**
  Pepper and Weitzman (2004) talk about four different communication styles which are shown in the table on page 28.

  Pepper and Weitzman (2004) explain that children may move between these styles, however most children will have a dominant communication style. A child's communication style can impact the speed at which he or she develops skills in a new language. Children with a more sociable communication style are likely to be more motivated to learn phrases in the new language to enable them to join in with the other children (e.g. 'my turn').

  Children who present with a more reluctant, passive or own agenda communication style are typically less motivated to attempt to use the new language, possibly remaining in the silent period for longer. Children with these styles may be slower to pick up a new language due to limited interactions with peers.

- **The well-being of the child**
  'Well-being is about feeling at ease, being spontaneous and free of emotional tensions, feeling self-confident, good about yourself and being resilient.' (Blank and Bevan, 2017)

  The better a child's well-being, the easier it will be for them to fulfil their potential in terms of additional language learning. A child who is not experiencing a good sense of well-being is likely to find it more challenging to learn new things, particularly a new language.

- **Proficiency in the child's first language**
  EAL learners who are new to your setting 'with a strong command of their first language and a developed range of concepts in that language are thus in a very favourable position to learn English.' (Gibbons, 1991)

  Gibbons (1991) explains that 'if you have sorted out the world in one language, it becomes much easier to sort it out again in a second language.' For this reason, it is vital to support each child's development

Chapter Two How children learn languages

of English as well as providing opportunities for them to continue to develop their home language. If a child has difficulties with their home language it will make it harder for them to learn and master a second/additional language. See Chapter eight for advice about supporting children who are struggling to learn English as an additional language.

- **Other barriers/SEND**
  Children who have difficulties in other areas such as attention and listening may find it more difficult to pick up a second language, even if their language skills are age appropriate in their first language. Similarly, children with social communication difficulties, perhaps autism spectrum disorder may also struggle with additional language learning. Additional medical conditions may also have an impact, for example a child with a physical disability who finds it more of a challenge to move around the setting might not be interacting with other children as much as he or she would have if it weren't for the physical disability.

Sociable communication style	• Starts interactions frequently • Responds readily when others initiate interactions • Tries to interact with others, even if they are not able to use words • Naturally takes the lead in interactions
Reluctant communication style	• Rarely starts interactions • Finds it easier to respond when someone else initiates the interactions • May need some time to 'warm' to a person before interacting with them
Passive communication style	• Rarely starts interactions • Often does not respond when someone initiates an interaction • Shows limited awareness of others
Own agenda communication style	• Plays alone the majority of the time • Will start interactions to get needs and wants met (e.g. when he or she wants something) but not often for other reasons • Often does not often respond when spoken to

(Based on Pepper and Weitzman, 2004)

Chapter Two How children learn languages

Differences between languages

There are over 300 languages spoken in the UK. It is useful to be aware of some of the key ways that one language can differ from another. If you have ever tried to learn another language yourself, you will probably know that languages don't just differ in terms of the vocabulary. Languages differ in many other ways.

Reflection

Do you have any experiences of learning a language at school?
Or were you exposed to more than one language yourself at home as a child?
If so, can you think of some ways that the languages that you know differ?
If you remember learning a new language at school, was this an easy experience?
Do you recall what was difficult about learning a new language?

As well as having different vocabularies and different sound systems, languages also vary in how words are put together to make phrases and sentences. Grammar is often a challenging element for anyone learning a new language!

Languages are different in terms of:

Vocabulary
- Each language has its own vocabulary.
- Not all languages have a word for everything that we have a word for. For example, there is no Punjabi word for 'coat', so they use the English word instead. Similarly, there is no Urdu word for 'nappy'. In English, we have a range of different greetings that can be used depending on the time of day (e.g. good morning, good afternoon). Many languages, including Urdu, Farsi and Punjabi don't have these.
- Similarly, we don't have a word for everything that all other languages have a single word for. For example, in English, the word 'grandmother' refers to a maternal grandmother or a paternal grandmother, whereas in Punjabi there are two different words for maternal grandmother and paternal grandmother.

Sentence structure
- Different languages follow different patterns for organising words in sentences.
- The order of words in sentences varies between languages. The English language has a subject, verb, object and word order (e.g. the boy kicked the ball). However, many languages have a different word order. In other languages the verb is often at the end of a sentence (e.g. in Bengali e.g. I to the shop go).

Use of function words
- Words such as 'is', 'are', 'was' and 'were' don't exist in some languages.
- There is no definite article ('the') in some languages.
- In English, we might say 'your dinner is on the table' however the word 'the' does not exist in all languages.
- Similarly the word 'a' does not exist in some languages (e.g. in English we might say 'I saw a mouse' whereas in some languages they would say 'I saw mouse').
- Prepositions occur after the noun in some languages. For example, in English we would say 'in the bin', whereas in some languages such as Urdu, they would say 'the bin in'.

Marking gender
- Some languages do not have different pronouns for males and females (he and she). For example, Finnish uses the same pronoun regardless of whether they are referring to a male or a female.
- Many languages, such as French, make a distinction between masculine and feminine items. In French, the words 'le' and 'la' both mean 'the', however 'le' is used for masculine items and 'la' is used for feminine items. There is no such distinction between masculine and feminine items in the English language.

The sounds in the language
- Be aware that some languages contain sounds that do not exist in the English language. In Spanish for example, they use a rolled 'r' sound that does not occur in English. Many languages also use vowels that we don't say in English.
- The English language also contains some sounds that do not exist in all other languages. Gujurati does not have the 'w' sound, for example.

Chapter Two How children learn languages

while before they have developed full competency in the English language, perhaps taking longer to master this element of the English language. (Shopen, 1979)

When it comes to pronunciation and development of speech sounds, some children who speak certain languages may struggle to pronounce the sounds that don't occur in their first language. For example, German speakers sometimes find it difficult to say the 'w' sound, instead replacing it with the 'v' sound (e.g. 'vater' instead of 'water'). The younger a child is when first exposed to a new language, the easier it will be to master the pronunciation of words that contain sounds that don't appear in their home language.

How do these differences impact on additional language learning?

Due to the many different features of each language, one EAL learner's attempts to use English may contain features that differ from another EAL learner's attempts.

What's more, some learners may struggle more with particular aspects of the English language that differ somewhat or do not exist in their home language. For example, a child with Finnish as a first language may have more difficulties learning the pronouns 'he' and 'she' than a child who speaks French as a first language. This is because, unlike English and French, the Finnish language does not have different pronouns for different genders. (Eckert & McConnell-Ginet, 2013)

Similarly, the differences in sentence structure and the use of function words in other languages can make it hard for children to learn a number of grammatical rules. For example, the Malagasy language (of Madagascar) has no auxiliary verbs (such as 'be', 'have' and 'do') therefore these children might miss out these words for a

Chapter Three Helping children to settle-in

For any child who is starting a new school, nursery or childcare setting, the settling-in period is a sensitive and crucial time. This time can be even more daunting for EAL learners, as they have the added uncertainty of being exposed to an unfamiliar language and in some cases a different culture. Settling-in procedures usually begin before a child starts at a setting and continue for as long as the child needs extra support and reassurance. This chapter is split into the following three sections:

- Part A - Before the child starts
- Part B - The child's first day
- Part C - The child's first few weeks.

There is practical advice on how to help a child settle-in, with a focus on the key person requirement 1: 'to help the child become familiar with the setting, offer a settled relationship for the child and build a relationship with their parents'. Further information on developing relationships with parents follows in Chapter six.

Part A – Before the child starts

When any new child starts at your setting, there will be a number of steps you need to take before their first day to help ensure that you are fully prepared for their arrival. For children who are new to the English language, there are essential details to gather about their own language experiences and abilities, as well as their background and culture.

Initial information sharing meeting

Information sharing with parents or carers is vital. Meet them before the child starts at your setting to gather all of the important information that will influence what you

Chapter Three Helping children to settle-in

do to help the child settle-in in the best possible way. As always with parents, information sharing is a two-way process. They need to be reassured that you and your setting will meet their child's needs, and they need to know what to expect.

This initial meeting is when your important relationship with parents begins. You may need to use an interpreter for this meeting if the parents or carers speak little or no English. See page 72 for tips about working with interpreters.

Ideally, this initial meeting would take place in the family home. This is so that you can see the child in their own environment where they feel most comfortable. You will hopefully be able to see the child interacting with their parents and playing as they usually would, using their home language. It also gives you some insight into home background, which will be useful when supporting the child.

A home visit is not always appropriate or possible in some cases. For example, some families live in poor quality housing which is often temporary and sometimes shared.

What's more, some parents may not understand the purpose of this home visit and instead may view this as an 'intrusive' visit. For example, families who have applied to be permanent residents in the UK are sometimes particularly cautious during the application process.

'A home visit to parents of learners who have EAL may appear strange and uncomfortable for religious, cultural or language issues, so it is best to be fully aware of the sensitivities involved.' (Sood and Mistry, 2015) An alternative would be to invite them into the setting for the pre-start information sharing meeting.

Topics to discuss with parents

You will of course be asking all of the usual questions that you ask parents of all new children around health, allergies, likes and dislikes, as well as discussing some key developmental milestones. In addition, it is important to ask parents of EAL learners additional questions to ensure that you have as much information as possible about their early experiences, use of language in the home, food they like and the home culture.

Most settings have a form to complete with parents for information gathering. It is important to include the questions specific for children learning EAL. There is a helpful checklist on pages 104-105 that you could use if you are developing a form for your setting.

Below are some of the key questions to ask parents of EAL learners:

What languages are spoken in the home?
- What language(s) has the child been exposed to at home?
- What language(s) do the adults use when speaking to the child?
- Do parents speak the same language to the child?
- What language do the parents/adults in the house use to speak to one another?
- If the child has siblings, what language is used between siblings?

Who lives in the home?
- If parents are living separately, what contact does the child have with each parent?
- Does the child have any siblings? If so, how many and are they younger or older?

Chapter Three Helping children to settle-in

- Do grandparents, aunties, uncles, cousins or any other relatives live with them? Be aware that extended family may live together as some cultures often have large numbers of people living under one roof.
- Is there anyone else who plays an important role in the child's life?

What religion does the family practice, if any?
- Does the child have any dietary requirements or other requirements that are religion based?

How able is the child in his or her home language(s)?
- Has the child started using words?
- Can parents give examples of the types of things their child might say?
- Do they use single words or are they joining words? Do they speak in longer phrases and sentences?
- Have parents ever had any concerns about their child's language development in their home language(s)?

How much exposure to English has the child had?
- Has the child had much exposure to English or will they be exposed to English properly for the first time when they start at the setting?

Does the child have previous experience of childcare or early years settings?
- What kind of setting have they spent time in and where?
- Will this be the first time the child is separated from the parents?

What opportunities has the child had for interaction with other children?
- Does the child have any siblings, other relatives, family friends or neighbours of a similar age with whom they spend a lot of time?
- Do they or have they ever attended any community groups such as 'stay and play' sessions?
- Does the child enjoy interacting with other children?

How would you describe the child's personality and temperament?
- Do they often get upset? Do they often have temper tantrums?
- What typically works to help them feel better when they get upset, frustrated or worried?

As well as completing forms when with parents, there are other ways of collecting more information that is going to help you plan a successful settling-in period for the child. Many settings use an '**All about me**' booklet for families to complete before their child starts the setting. See page 103 for an example of an 'All about me' template. This can be completed in the language that the child knows best, so that it is meaningful for him/her. It can then be translated into English by the parent or someone else such as a friend, family member or perhaps someone at your setting.

Key vocabulary in the child's home language

If there is no one in the setting who speaks the same language as the child, ask parents how to say some essential words and phrases in their home language. Make a note next to the words to help you remember how to pronounce them.

'Ask parents for a list of basic phrases including greetings, basic needs and so on, and how to pronounce them.' (New Arrivals Excellence Programme Guidance, 2007)

English as an additional language (EAL) in practice

Chapter Three Helping children to settle-in

On pages 108-111 there are lists of key vocabulary in some of the most commonly spoken languages in the UK, with pronunciation tips.

Information to give to parents

Parents need a clear picture of what to expect when their child joins the setting in order to prepare and reassure their child before they begin, and in the early days of settling-in. Giving parents this clear picture is also important for establishing trust, which is essential for relationship building.

Below are some of the most important topics to discuss with parents and key information to give them.

Provide information about the setting
- Be aware that educational settings vary considerably between countries.
- Parents of new arrivals may not be familiar with the education system in the UK, and in particular the play-based curriculum in the Early Years Foundation Stage.
- When discussing this with parents, be aware that cultural differences exist in attitudes towards play (see pages 62-63).

Discuss the role of the key person
- Tell the parents who the child's key person is and explain what this means. Be aware that this way of working will be completely unfamiliar to some people.
- It can be reassuring for parents to know that their child's key person will help the child to settle during their initial days and weeks, but will also offer an ongoing supportive relationship with the child and parents.

Ensure that they are clear on everyday details about the running of the setting
- Clearly explain and where possible give written information in their home language about practical details such as start time, pick up time, where exactly to drop off and pick up their child from, as well as what will be offered in the way of drinks and snacks, etc.

Provide parents with any specially prepared resources, such as welcome packs in the relevant language wherever possible
- You will have given them a lot of information so it is often reassuring for parents to know that they have much of this information available in written or audio form.
- You may also direct them to your setting's website if there is useful or additional information online.

Discuss the importance of the child's home language
- Ensure that parents understand the importance of continuing to speak the child's first language. Explain that continuing to speak and develop their home language will help them to learn new things more easily and it will also make it easier for them to learn English. See pages 15-16 for a more in-depth explanation of its importance.

It is also important to have a discussion about the parents' **preferred method of communication**. For parents who will drop off and pick up their children every day, you will have many opportunities for regular discussions. For parents who will not be doing this, you may have to make alternative arrangements for regular liaison. Some parents will be happy to be contacted by phone, whereas some prefer to be contacted by email or through a communication book, for example.

Chapter Three Helping children to settle-in

If parents are not able to speak English, they may have a relative or a friend who can support with communication when necessary. See page 72 for advice about interpreting if parents do not have access to someone who is able to translate for them.

Case Study: Initial information sharing meeting

Child's name: Urszula
Child's age: 2 years, 6 months
First language: Polish
Background information: Urszula was born in Poland. She moved to London with her family at the age of 2 years and 3 months. Her parents are both Polish and they all speak Polish to one another at home. She has one younger sibling who is 18 months younger than her. Urszula started at the age of 2 years and 5 months old.

Urszula's key person and another staff member did a home visit to carry out the information sharing meeting with Urszula's mother. Urszula's mother is relatively proficient in English so she did not require an interpreter for the initial meeting.

Feedback from Urszula's mother about the initial parent meeting:
- The staff showed me lots of pictures of what they do in nursery
- Urszula enjoyed playing with her toys in the same room
- The staff gave me a welcome pack with lots of useful information about Urszula's nursery
- It was good to have the opportunity to ask lots of questions.

Part B - The child's first day

Planning for the child's first day

As the child's key person, there will be things to consider further and resources to prepare following the initial parent information sharing meeting. Here are some ideas:

Prepare a selection of visuals
- Gather a selection of photographs or pictures of things such as the toilet, water, etc. that the child can point to or bring to you if needed. These could be attached with a split pin to make a 'communication fan' or they could be attached to a board on the wall with velcro.
- Ensure that these visuals are kept in a specific place in your setting so that the child can access them at any time.

Set up a visual timetable
- Visual timetables are vital for supporting EAL children to settle-in and to reassure them about what will be happening and in what order throughout the day. See page 49 for more information about setting up and using a visual timetable in your setting.

Adapt your environment
- There is a whole chapter about how to alter the environment to ease children's settling-in and help them feel relaxed (See Chapter Four: Creating a Suitable Environment).

Chapter Three Helping children to settle-in

Consider the toys, activities and resources that will appeal to the child
- Think about the information that the parent gave you at the pre-start meeting about the child's interests.
- You may already have a selection of resources and materials that are related to the child's likes and interests or you may need to do some gathering of resources and materials if the child's interests are less common.
- Perhaps think about ordering a few dual-language books in the child's home language if you do not already have any in your setting. See pages 47 and 61 for information about the value of dual-language books.

Learn a selection of key words and phrases in the child's home language
- You will hopefully have gathered a list of essential words from the child's parents at the initial information sharing meeting or from the resources section at the back of the book.

> ### Practitioner perspective
> "We recently had a new arrival start at our nursery and I am the child's key person. I found it actually really useful to learn some key words in Albanian (the child's home language) so that I could use these with the child when he started. I think it helped the child to develop a relationship with me and made him feel more at ease."

What to do on the child's first day

Smile and relax!
- In order for the child to feel relaxed, the adults around them need to feel relaxed.
- Remember, entering a completely new place can be daunting for anyone, even adults. Being in a new setting where everyone else speaks a completely unfamiliar language is even more daunting!

Make sure all adults are pronouncing the child's name correctly
- This will show the child that their identity is important and will make the child feel more welcome.

- Names are important! They are unique to every individual therefore they give us a sense of identity. In many cases, names have a cultural or religious significance and they often signify gender. There may be a special meaning behind a child's name so it is also important to check with parents before shortening a child's name.

Reassure parents
- Reassure parents that the settling-in period is flexible and they can stay for as long as needed to help settle their child in the new environment.
- Remember that it is normal for parents to be anxious about leaving their child in a new setting, particularly when the child doesn't speak the main language spoken in the setting. During a child's initial few days, successful ways of reassuring parents often include showing them videos or photos of their child participating in activities and having fun. In some cases, phone calls to parents to reassure them after they have dropped off their child may be appropriate and helpful.

Chapter Three Helping children to settle-in

Use the visual timetable!
- Show the child what will be happening throughout the day. Once an activity has finished, ensure that the appropriate picture is removed from the timetable. Children often enjoy taking it in turns to update the visual timetable and placing the appropriate picture into a 'finished box' for example. See page 49 for more information about visual timetables.
- A child can look at the visual timetable at any time to see what will be happening next. Visual timetables also help to give children an idea of how long is left until home time, which is often reassuring for children who are not able to speak the main language of the setting, particularly during the initial days and weeks.

Set up a buddy system
- 'Find a buddy for the child who either shares the same language and/or has strong social skills.' (Soni, 2013)
- Depending on age, you could identify a child or a couple of children who will play a part in supporting an EAL learner to settle-in to your setting. They will be able to help the child to follow the everyday routines for example.

Be sensitive to the child's emotions
- Use information gathered from the pre-start visit about how best to soothe the child, along with your usual successful ways to distract and cheer up a child such as cuddles, a quiet cosy space, soft toys or items of interest. If there is someone in the setting who can speak the child's home language, using them to help put the child at ease can be very reassuring.

Use bilingual staff and peers (or use key words and phrases in the child's home language)
- Hearing and being able to use their home language can really make the settling-in process easier for a child with no English. As well as reassuring them and making them feel more at ease, it also enables them to communicate key messages.
- If nobody in the setting shares a language in common with the child, it is important that the child's key person makes an extra effort to use some key words and phrases in the child's home language.

- Gibbons (1991) explains that this can help to 'lessen the trauma and alienation children may experience in a new environment, surrounded by an unknown language.' When children are more comfortable and at ease, they are in a better position to learn, explore, play and communicate.

Give the child time and space
- Practitioners need to 'give the new learners space to grow confident and adjust to the English learning culture' (Sood and Mistry, 2015).
- Children need the opportunity to explore in their own time, but also to know that a familiar adult is there if and when they need them.
- Remember, at first a child may not understand what is expected of them, particularly if the adults in the setting look and behave in ways that are different to what the child is used to.

Chapter Three Helping children to settle-in

Case Study: Abdi

Child's name: Abdi
First language: Somali
Child's age: 3 years, 2 months

Abdi has recently started at nursery. At home, Somali language is used. Abdi's parents have lived in the UK for 6 years. Abdi's father can speak some English however his mother does not speak any English. Abdi has had limited exposure to English, other than when in shops etc. in the community.

Abdi's parents have no other family nearby however they have a few friends from their religious setting. They know two other families who attend the same nursery as Abdi. Abdi enjoys playing with the children of these family friends and will chat in Somali to them.

Abdi's mum reported that it was lovely to see the train set out when they arrived on Abdi's first day, as he loves trains. She felt that this made it easier for Abdi to get settled on his first day, and stopped him getting too upset when she left him there.

Abdi's mum also reported that there was another boy who spoke Somali in the nursery so it was great that they were able to play and talk together in Somali.

Abdi's mum said that, after the information sharing meeting she felt relaxed as she knew that the staff were very caring and her son would be happy at nursery.

Part C - The child's first few weeks

During an EAL learner's first few weeks and months in a new setting, it is important to do all of the following:

Provide ongoing opportunities for the child to use their home language

- Ensure that the child has many opportunities to use his or her home language, particularly if there is nobody who speaks the child's first language in the setting.

- There are many ideas about how to provide ongoing opportunities for the child to hear and use their home language in Chapter five.

Continue to be aware of the emotions of the child

- It may take a while for the child to feel at home in the setting, as language learning is a long and tricky process! So the child may need a lot of emotional support for a few months whilst they get used to the new language sounds, nursery routines, food, people and a whole host of unfamiliar experiences.

Be conscious not to underestimate the child

- Children who are EAL learners are just as capable as any other children, therefore 'the learning experiences planned for them should be no less challenging.' (Primary National Strategy, 2007)
- EAL learners need to be challenged cognitively on a day-to-day basis in order to reach their potential (Soni, 2013). Be sure that you are offering them opportunities to continue to explore and learn using all of their senses and to make a range of discoveries on a daily basis.

Chapter Three Helping children to settle-in

Have fun playing together
- Join in with the child's play and have fun together making noises (e.g. 'choo choo', 'meow', 'oink, oink'). This is a lovely way to interact without the child feeling pressured to attempt to use the new language. You can use simple language to comment on what is happening during the play (e.g. 'wow...you're building!', '1, 2, 3!', 'crash...uh ohh...it's broken'). This helps the child to learn words in the new language, again without putting pressure on the child. There is a whole chapter about how to interact with EAL learners (see Chapter Five: Adult-child interaction).

Make books come alive!
- As well as making story time more exciting and interactive, using props such as puppets and story sacks can really help children to understand what is being said.
- Dual-language books are also fantastic resources that can be used in a range of ways to support the EAL learners in your setting. See page 61 for more information.

Have fun singing together
- Songs and rhymes are often the first vehicle for a child's attempts to use a new language and their repetitive nature makes them easy for children to learn. Include songs and nursery rhymes in your sessions several times a day in different situations, for example during group time as well as when in the garden or during tidy up time.
- Speak to parents about the songs that the child knows in their home language. Can you learn these and sing these in your setting?

Facilitate peer interaction
- Playing and interacting with other children is one of the best ways children learn a new language.
- Chapter four talks about different areas within your setting that promote peer interaction (e.g. home corner, quiet area, areas for discoveries).
- If you have an area for discoveries outside (e.g. with magnifying glasses and plastic bugs), perhaps think about sending the child out with two or three other childen who are likely to interact with the child in a positive way.
- Ensure that resources and materials available will excite and capture the attention and imagination of the children. When children are excited about an activity they are usually more keen to share their excitement with others.
- Supporting a child to join in with peers who are involved in activities that don't rely on spoken language can be a great way to facilitate peer interaction. Physical activities are great for this!
- See page 58 for plenty more ideas about how to promote interaction between peers when you have a child who is new to English in your setting.

Supporting a child who is going through the silent period
- If you have a child who is going through a silent period, ensuring that you interact appropriately with them is crucial. See page 59 for practical advice about how best to interact with children during the silent period.

Chapter Three Helping children to settle-in

Case Study: Settling-in period

Child's name: Alban
Child's age: 3 years, 1 month
First language: Albanian
Background information: Alban was born in the UK however, he has only been exposed to Albanian at home.

When he joined the setting, he entered very happily on his first day. There was another child in the setting who spoke Albanian and they both spent a lot of time together playing and chatting.

They particularly enjoyed making discoveries together outside.

After a couple of weeks, Alban started to use English, initially through songs at group time. He learnt some key phrases that he attempted to use with a range of peers (e.g. 'my turn'). Soon after he began to use new words every day when playing.

Case Study: Settling-in period

Child's name: Aisha
Child's age: 4 years, 2 months
First language: Somali
Background information: Aisha and her family moved from Somalia to London and Aisha started in reception not long after arriving in the UK. This was the first exposure that she had had to the English language.

During her first few days in reception she was highly emotional, crying much of the time. There were no other children or staff members who spoke the same language in the setting.

When she was upset, her key person took her to the cosy area or the sensory tent. She found that sensory toys helped Aisha to calm down.

Her key person made a conscious effort to ensure that she was providing necessary emotional support during the settling-in period.

When she could foresee that situations may be a little challenging or overwhelming for Aisha, she considered more suitable alternatives. For example, on her first few days in reception, rather than sending Aisha to assembly, she and a couple of other children were supported in the outdoor play area instead.

Aisha went through a silent period for approximately 6 weeks. She joined in with the actions of songs during this silent period and then first attempted to use English words in her attempts to sing her favourite rhyme of Baa Baa Black Sheep.

Practitioner perspective

"We have lots of children who are learning EAL in our nursery. Some of them come in happily and naturally pick up the language in their own time but others find it a bit more difficult to settle-in. We find that it helps to think about the child's interests and provide them with resources and toys that engage and motivate them as this allows them be more relaxed."

Chapter Four Creating a suitable environment

'…the environment of the setting can be optimized to enhance the learning experiences of the children learning EAL.' (Soni, 2013)

The EYFS Statutory Framework (2017) states that 'children learn and develop well in enabling environments'. This chapter looks at what makes an 'enabling environment'; it explores the features of inclusive and communication friendly early years settings, highlighting changes that can be made in order to create an environment in which EAL learners can thrive.

There are several key factors that should always be taken into consideration in a setting where EAL learners attend. These factors include: the types of spaces available in the setting, the familiarity and consistency of the environment, the suitability of play materials and resources available and finally, the way in which all cultures, ethnicities and languages are represented. These key factors will each be explored in turn.

Communication Friendly Spaces (Jarman, 2006)

In any early years setting, it is important to carefully consider your environment to ensure that it is safe, functional and practical. However, this is by no means all that we are aiming for; it is of utmost importance to ensure that the setting supports the learning and development of all children, regardless of their background. All settings should be 'prepared in such a way that all children's language can be developed in positive and creative ways through your inclusive practices and environments.'
(Brodie and Savage, 2015)

Chapter Four Creating a suitable environment

Elizabeth Jarman (2006) developed the concept of 'communication friendly spaces'. She explains that communication and social interactions can be impacted by noise, light and storage, and how resources can be used in creative ways to capture the interest of the children and to promote communication. Jarman considers 'softness and homeliness, open-ended resources, seasonal resources, recycled and re-purposed materials, according to children's fascinations.' (Blank and Bevan, 2017)

Jarman argues that the environment impacts on the way children feel and behave. 'We are all consciously and subconsciously affected by our environment. It can affect our thoughts, feelings and behaviours'. (Jarman, 2009) This is particularly relevant to EAL learners, especially when they are new to a setting, as the more relaxed and at ease a child feels, the more likely they are to learn.

Making the environment suitable for EAL learners

For children who are learning English as an additional language, there are several factors that should be considered to help them thrive. It is vital that the four key factors listed below are at the forefront of your mind when arranging the environment:

1) The types of spaces within the setting
2) The types of materials and resources available
3) The familiarity and predictability of the setting
4) Ensure that the setting is visually accepting of all backgrounds, cultures, ethnicities and languages.

These four factors are discussed in turn below, with practical practitioner tips and case studies from settings.

1 - The types of spaces within your setting

Jarman (2006) highlights the importance of having different types of spaces for different types of activities within early years settings. Having a range of different types of spaces benefits all children, not just children learning English as an additional language.

We know that children learn and begin to use a new language best when they are interacting with other

children in natural play situations. There are spaces that we can create that naturally facilitate and encourage these positive peer interactions and everyday play conversations.

Areas for being active and physical
- 'Young children learn well through being physical, since being physical is an inbuilt urge for them.' (Blank and Bevan, 2017)
- Open spaces encourage children to be physical. The size of the outdoor space available will of course vary in every setting. Regardless of size, ensure that there is an open space free of equipment, to enable the children to run around, race one another and pretend to be a plane or a bird for example.
- It is well known that being active gives us a 'feel good factor'. If children have the opportunity to engage in physical activities every day, they will experience a regular rush of endorphins, which are known as 'feel good hormones'. This is likely to have a positive impact on their overall well-being. A large part of supporting EAL children to communicate in early years settings is about ensuring that the child feels comfortable and relaxed enough to do so, so

Chapter Four Creating a suitable environment

taking steps to ensure the well-being of the child can only be a positive thing in terms of promoting communication.

- Many settings have fixed equipment such as climbing frames and slides; these are often very popular with the children and can help them develop social communication skills such as turn-taking, in a very natural way. At the same time they will come to understand terms like 'you go first', 'my turn' and prepositional language such as 'under', 'through', 'on top', etc.
- Children also enjoy using portable equipment such as scooters, trikes, hoola hoops and balls which also naturally promote social interaction and lots of meaningful language. EAL learners will soon understand words such as 'stop', 'go', 'fast' when on wheeled toys, and some simple verbs such as 'catch' and 'kick' when playing with balls. Varying the portable equipment that you put out from day to day can be an easy way to promote interactions between peers, as they explore the new items together, perhaps teaching one another how to use items and then showing off their new skills.

Areas that encourage exploring

- Children are natural explorers. They learn through exploring and experiencing different things with all of their senses. Some children will have endless fantastic opportunities to explore when in the care of their parents or main carer, however for others, these opportunities can be limited.
- You may have an area for exploring inside, with items hidden in sands trays for example, or water trays with various types of containers and watering cans. You may also have a heuristic play area. Heuristic play is 'play where babies and toddlers explore natural materials and play with them in any way they wish' (Blank and Bevan, 2017). These activities are multisensory and therefore promote exploration.
- Outside is a fantastic place to explore with so much wildlife and the exciting natural world. As there is so much to see and find in the great outdoors it is particularly conducive to language learning. (Sargent, 2016)
- Materials that facilitate and encourage exploring include magnifying glasses (e.g. for minibeast hunting), binoculars, and outfits (e.g. explorer

Chapter Four Creating a suitable environment

- The home corner is often an area in which small groups of children enjoy playing with one another. It is worthwhile spending time making the home corner a 'homely' place, using tablecloths, cosy seats and dolls' beds, etc. For some children who are new to the English language, the home corner is considered to be a safe space for them to start interacting with other children who they feel comfortable with, whether they are using words or non-verbal communication.

Areas for being calm

- 'Children need to rest, withdraw from the busy play area, have time alone, sit with you and play, chat with a friend, be calm, calm down.' (Blank and Mathews, 2017)
- Calm areas are particularly important for children who are new to English. This is because being in a new language environment can cause children to feel a range of emotions, as well as being incredibly tiring. These children may therefore want to move away from other children for some calm time at various points throughout the day.
- It is essential that all early years settings have a comfortable area that allows time for being calm, perhaps with soft chairs, or bean bags, cushions and

costumes). You can also plant items (e.g. placing conkers and acorns on the floor outside) to ensure that children make exciting discoveries.
- If a child experiences something exciting for the first time, they will often want to communicate this with someone. Children have an inbuilt urge to share their excitement and experiences with others. This is why areas for exploring can be so beneficial in promoting communication and social interaction.

Smaller areas to encourage peer interaction

- For some children, interacting with other children is easier and comes more naturally in small spaces, for example in a den or a play house. Children progress with language and communication through playing and talking with other children so it is important to have small spaces of some kind in your setting. Children who speak the same language often choose to retreat to smaller spaces and chat together in the common language. (Sargent, 2016) Create indoor and outdoor hiding spaces and dens using tents, blankets, willow tunnels and trees.

Chapter Four Creating a suitable environment

soft toys. Some settings have tents that they use as calm, comfortable areas. Regardless of where in your setting this is, it should be a nice relaxing place for a child to spend time.

Distraction-free areas

- Early years settings are often busy and noisy. Elks and McLachlan (2016) also recommend having a 'quiet, low distraction area' when children can concentrate on an activity away from the hustle and bustle of the main play areas. This is essential if you have EAL learners in your setting, as it is more difficult to focus on an activity that is in a new language. This area should not replace a calm and comfortable place to rest or relax, instead it is an additional quiet space for children to engage in activities with less going on around them.

As highlighted already, having these areas benefits all children. Below is an example of how a child who was exposed to English for the first time when he started nursery, made use of the different spaces depending on his mood and his tiredness levels, etc.

Case Study: Arian

Child's name: Arian
Age: 3 years

Arian recently moved to the UK from Albania where he lived from birth. At home, Arian and his parents all speak Albanian.

When he first started at nursery, the sensory tent was a comfort for him. He was also comforted by soft toys in the 'calm corner'. During his first few days he would spend some time outside exploring, however he would typically come back to the calm corner or the sensory tent after a short period of time outside.

After four weeks in his nursery, Arian only uses the sensory tent and the 'calm corner' very occasionally, as he is outside exploring most of the time. He also enjoys being around the other children and will interact with them using non-verbal communication and sometimes single words or short phrases. Sometimes towards the end of a session when he is tired, Arian will bring himself inside and take some time for himself in a quieter area.

Chapter Four Creating a suitable environment

Ensure that multicultural items are available for play and learning

- It is important to ensure that there are resources readily available that reflect each child's culture and background.
- 'Make sure images and objects reflect the student's culture, e.g. foods, types of transport, housing, tools and utensils, textile designs.' (Washbourne, 2011) For example, in the home corner it is appropriate to have toy foods reflecting world cuisine as well as a range of utensils and cutlery such as chop sticks. Tablecloths and dressing up clothing should also feature a range of patterns and designs from around the world.
- This is important as children may feel more comfortable engaging in play with resources and materials that are familiar to them. In addition, it shows that the setting values each child's culture and background, which will support each child in developing their sense of identity as well as their self-esteem.

It is clear from the case study on page 45 that children seek different environments at different times of the day, depending on a number of factors, including how tired they are, how they are feeling and whether or not they simply feel the need for a break away from the other children to wind down a little. As a key person, you will play a part in supporting the children to make these transitions from one area to another when appropriate.

2 - Types of materials and resources available

'In the early years, EAL learners need much the same as other young children, namely active, hands-on activities than enable them to link language to first-hand experience.'
(Sargent, 2016)

Provide a good range of interesting resources and experiences, so that children are motivated to express themselves in a range of different situations. This is important because 'different play situations lend themselves to different vocabulary.' (Blank and Bevan, 2017)

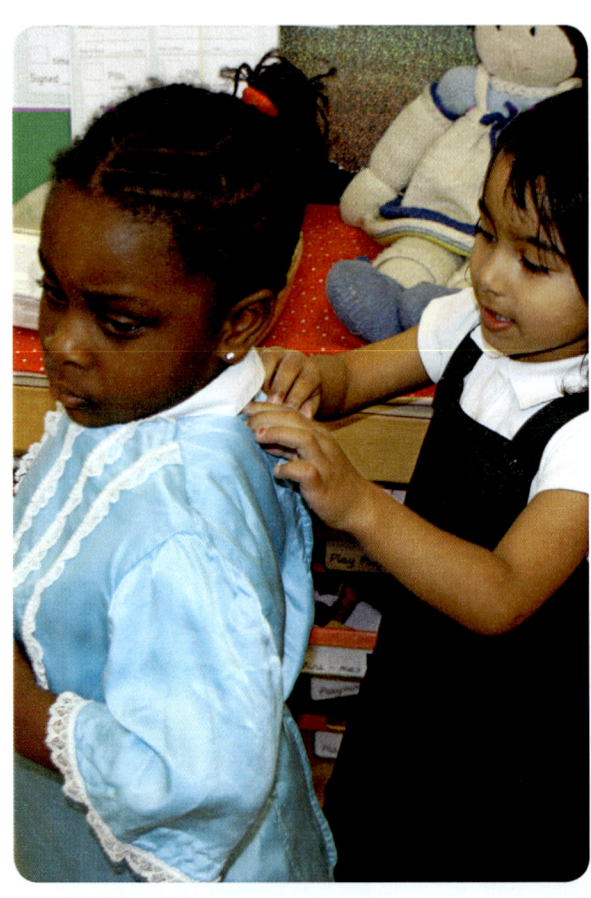

Chapter Four Creating a suitable environment

Example of a cultural difference in household items

Some families do not use kettles to boil water at home, instead they boil water in a pan. A child who has never had experience of a kettle at home is more likely to pretend to make a hot drink in the home corner if there is a pan that they can pretend with, as this reflects what they have experience of and seeing at home.

Well-resourced book area with dual-language books

- Dual-language picture books are simple books that have text in two languages. So as well as English words, there will also be the same words but in another language, for example Polish or Somali. See page 61 for more information about dual-language books, including examples of how they can be used with the EAL learners in your setting.
- If you are in a setting that sees high numbers of EAL learners, are there any languages that are more common? If so, you may consider buying a range of books in the most commonly spoken languages and a smaller selection to reflect the less common languages.
- In the case study setting in Greater London, a high proportion of the EAL learners are from families who speak Somali, so they have purchased a range of Somali-English dual-language books to reflect this. Of course, they also have dual-language books to represent all of the languages spoken by the children in their setting.

Practitioner perspective

"Dual-language books are fantastic! Recently, I observed one of the older children in the nursery sitting with a little boy who hasn't been at the nursery very long. They were looking at a dual-language picture book together and she was naming the items in English for him. He was naming some in his first language. It was a lovely interaction."

Resources related to the interests of the children

- Resources should be related to the interests of the children. During an EAL learner's initial settling-in period, ensuring that resources are related to his or her interests is essential to help the child settle-in well and feel comfortable, happy and motivated to explore and learn.

3 - The familiarity and practicability of the setting

'When children come into a setting they like to know what to expect. If things are familiar and predictable they will feel confident, relaxed and able to play and learn.' (Blank and Mathews, 2017)

This is of particular importance for children who are new to English due to the high levels of emotions that they may be experiencing such as worry, confusion and anxiety. Familiarity and predictability can help to reduce the intensity of these emotions and help children to feel more at ease.

Chapter Four Creating a suitable environment

- Over time, the selection of resources and materials within each of the designated areas should be added to or changed according to interests, observations of learning, seasonal events and times of year, to ensure that there is an element of surprise and excitement within this predictable environment. This will help to capture the imagination of the children and to extend their learning. (Blank and Mathews, 2017)

Resources in specific places

- If children know where items are kept, this will enable them to access what they would like to play with at their own pace. This is particularly helpful for children who are new to English who may not have the skills to request certain items verbally.

Photographs accompanying any labels

- Clearly labelling boxes and baskets containing resources with photographs or pictures can help children to identify where resources go more easily.

Reflection

Can you think of some ways that you can make the environment more familiar and predictable for the children?

Below are some of the main ways in which we can make a setting more predictable for a child:

Areas designated for specific activities

- For children to feel at home in their setting they need to know what to expect. Having specific activities (such as construction, painting and book reading) in designated areas can help them settle-in more easily. They will be able to go straight to their activity of choice without trying to work out what is where each day when they enter the setting. 'This is often called 'continuous provision'. It is important to enable children to feel at home and to have some ownership of their setting.' (Blank and Mathews, 2017)

Chapter Four Creating a suitable environment

Visual timetables

Visual timetables are used to show children what will be happening throughout the day and in what order.

Clear photos or pictures should be used and placed on display in the order of events.

Once an activity has finished, the picture should be removed from the visual timetable. Children should be involved in updating the visual timetable with adult support. Perhaps the children in your setting could take it in turns to place a picture in a 'finished box' once the activity is over. Updating the timetable in this way makes it more meaningful for the children. They will be able to look at the timetable at any point in the day and be able to see what to expect next.

Visual timetables are particularly useful for children who have limited English and who are in a completely new environment. If an adult tells a child 'it's story time' while pointing to the story time visual, the child will be able to understand what is about to happen, even if they do not yet understand any English at all.

Visual timetables also give children some indication of how long is left before their parents or carers will be returning to collect them. This can be very reassuring for new starters.

Group time

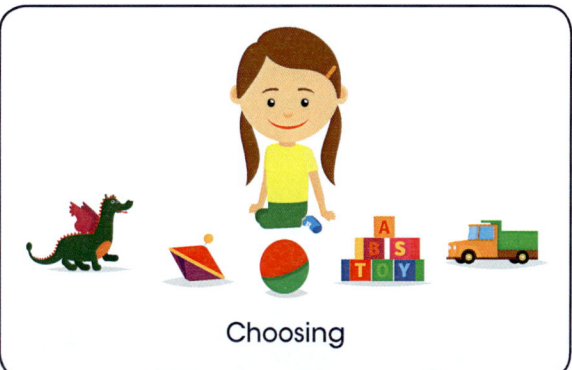
Choosing

Snack time

Story time

Outside

Home time

Chapter Four Creating a suitable environment

Make other visuals available for children to use

- If the child has access to a range of picture resources that he or she can use to get a message across to others, this can make a child feel more relaxed and enable them to communicate more successfully. You may have a board with a range of photographs of things that the child might want to request attached with velcro. The child can then help themselves to the picture card that reflects what they want to say, and bring it to an adult.

Reduce distractions and unnecessary background noise

- New environments can be a little overwhelming for children at times, particularly when they are submerged into a new culture where a new language is spoken. There is often a lot to take in visually when entering an early years setting. Reducing background noise where possible can make it easier for a child to relax, particularly if the child is sensitive to noise.

Doing all of the above will make the environment feel somewhat more familiar and predictable. This will make children feel more relaxed and at ease. The more relaxed and at ease a child is in a setting, the easier it will be for them to make progress with their language and communication development.

4 - Ensure that your setting is visually inclusive of all backgrounds, cultures, ethnicities and languages

'Whatever their background, each learner and their family needs to feel as welcomed as possible by the setting embracing their culture.'
(Mistry and Sood, 2015)

Your physical environment plays a big part in making everyone feel valued. If children and their parents see their background and culture reflected in a positive way in their surroundings, this helps them to gain a sense of belonging and to feel valued. (Washbourne, 2011)

Chapter Four Creating a suitable environment

Case Study: Rifat

Child's name: Rifat
Child's age: 4 years, 5 months
Home language: Bengali
Background information: Rifat was born in Bangladesh. He started in a school nursery when he and his family moved to the UK, when Rifat was 3 and a half years old. He is now in reception.

Rifat's mother reported the following:

Rifat loves the dual-language books at school and he often brings one home so that we can read them together in our home language. He also tells me that he likes pretending to make snacks in the home corner.

The teachers recognise our religious celebrations. Rifat has taken in photographs of our Eid celebrations and shown them at school. His teacher loved seeing the photos of our celebrations. Rifat has taught his class some simple songs in Bengali and the children sing them together.

Case Study: Communication friendly setting

One school nursery in the West Midlands caters for children who speak 12 different languages. They have the following areas:

Inside:
- Well resourced book corner with a range of dual-language books
- The 'cosy corner' which, as the name suggests, is complete with cushions, bean bags, soft chairs and blankets
- Sensory tent with a bubble tube and coloured lights
- Tabled areas
- Carpet area
- Creative area
- Home corner
- Mirrored area
- Heuristic play area with tarpaulin covering.

Outside:
- Large open space
- Permanent climbing equipment
- Exploration area (resources and materials in this area change regularly)
- Portable equipment such as bikes, trikes and hoops
- Covered area with outdoor tents.

Other information:
The welcome pack has been translated into several languages. They use pupil interpreters from key stage 2 to help EAL children settle-in when appropriate. Photographs are shared on an online platform. Both nursery staff and parents/carers can upload to this platform.

Wall displays should be reflective of cultures and languages

- Displays should contain photographs and pictures of children from a diverse range of backgrounds, doing a whole host of different activities to reflect the background of the EAL learners in your setting.

Signage in various languages

- The signs around your setting should contain messages in multiple languages.

Chapter Five Adult-child interaction

'As early years practitioners, we are entrusted to care for and educate babies and young children' (Blank and Bevan, 2017). Many babies, toddlers and young children spend a large chunk of their day in your care, therefore, along with parents, you play an absolutely pivotal role in supporting their communication and language development.

The way you interact and the quality of your interactions with the children in your setting influences their opportunities to communicate and can also facilitate language and communication development (Elks and McLachlan, 2016).

This chapter therefore discusses how best to interact with EAL learners, including babies who are learning two languages at the same time, as well as slightly older children who are learning English after developing skills in a home language.

What does the EYFS say?

'Practitioners must respond to each child's emerging needs and interests, guiding their development through warm, positive interaction.' (EYFS, 2017)

The EYFS recognises that 'communication and language development involves giving children opportunities to experience a rich language environment; to develop their confidence and skills in expressing themselves; and to speak and listen in a range of situations.' (EYFS, 2017)

Children progress with language learning and communication development through listening to others, watching others and of course through meaningful

Chapter Five Adult-Child Interaction

interactions with other children and adults. This is true for monolingual children, those learning more than one language simultaneously, and those learning an additional language after learning a first.

As well as promoting EAL learners' language development in their home language and in English, our interactions with babies, toddlers and children must also aim to support their social communication skills. Key social communication skills that we want to support children to develop in the early years include:

- Smiling back when smiled at
- Responding appropriately when greeted
- Initiating interactions appropriately
- Joining in with others
- Taking-turns and sharing
- Making appropriate eye contact.

Adult-child interaction is all about the way adults interact with babies, toddlers and children. It is about far more than just the words that are spoken; it is also about body language, facial expressions, tone of voice and much more.

'As a significant role model, and to have a positive impact, you (the practitioner) must pay attention to your language, body language, behaviour and feelings when with the children.' (Blank and Bevan, 2017)

Key principles for quality adult-child interaction

Below are six key principles that are crucial to ensure quality adult-child interaction and to promote the language and communication development of all children:

1) Provide good models
2) Be responsive
3) Be positive
4) Consider the situation
5) Consider ages and stages
6) Consider individual circumstances.

1) Provide good models

The statutory framework states that children require a language rich environment. In order to learn a new word, either in their first language or an additional language, children need to hear the word being used in meaningful situations.

Good quality adult-child interaction occurs when adults talk to babies and children during everyday activities, at a level that suits the child. Tune in to the child and use simple language to name the things that the child is looking at or taking an interest in. Repetition is key in adult-child interaction, as children need to hear a word many times before they can pick up the word, whether this is in their first language or an additional language. In order to progress with their language, children need to hear language that is a little bit more advanced than their own.

Children unconsciously mirror or copy actions and behaviours that they see others doing as we have 'mirror neurons' in our brain. These 'mirror neurons' play a part in many areas of child development, particularly in language and communication development (Rizzolatti et al., 2002). So in order for children to develop good social communication skills, we need to be demonstrating these skills to them. Greet other staff members in a friendly manner in front of the children, demonstrate how to take turns and physically get down to the child's level so that you can make eye contact with them more easily.

Chapter Five Adult-Child Interaction

2) Be responsive

Most young children are very social little beings who enjoy interactions with warm, positive and responsive adults. Responding to the communication of a baby, toddler or young child teaches them that their efforts and attempts to communicate are valued, making them more likely to communicate more with you and with others. It also strengthens the bond that the child has with you. This involves tuning in to not only the noises and words that the child says, but also their non-verbal communication such as their facial expression and body language.

'Secure attachment between parent and child develops through parents' responsiveness to their child's communication, meaning babies and children are more ready to learn'. (The Communication Trust, 2011)

3) Be positive

The EYFS recognises the importance of 'warm, positive interactions' to support the development of babies and young children. Non-verbal communication (e.g. facial expressions and body language) is incredibly powerful. It is thought that over 50% of messages are conveyed through non-verbal communication (Elks and McLachlan, 2016). A relaxed or smiling face is much more comforting and approachable than a stern, cross expression. Of course, your expression will vary depending on the situation and the behaviours of the children. However, reacting in a positive way to achievements that children make, as well as responding to mistakes in an understanding way are both incredibly important in supporting children's development in communication and language as well as the other prime areas, particularly personal, social and emotional development, which is a crucial area of development for EAL learners.

4) Consider the situation

Adult-child interactions vary from one situation to the next. For example, during story time you will be communicating with the children in a very animated and enthusiastic manner, compared to during nap time or when comforting a child who is upset. Adapt the language that you use and your communication style to suit the situation.

5) Consider ages and stages

The way you interact with the babies and children in your setting will vary depending on their age. For babies, you will be using very simple language. However, as they progress through the early years and develop in the prime area of learning and development, the way you interact with them will change.

6) Consider individual circumstances

As we know, all children develop and progress at different rates. When working with young children you will also need to consider individual circumstances, such as the length of time that an EAL learner has been exposed to English. The way you interact with a child who is going through a silent period will be very different to the way you interact with a child who is confidently and competently using English as an additional language. Similarly, the way you interact with children who have communication difficulties will also be different to the way you interact with a child with advanced language and communication skills.

Chapter Five Adult-Child Interaction

Interacting with simultaneous learners (under 3 years)

Interacting with babies

There are few differences in the way that you interact with babies who are simultaneously learning two languages, compared to the way you would interact with a monolingual baby.

> 'Connect with babies and toddlers by copying their noises and facial expressions; by doing so you are expressing pleasure in their company by acknowledging and valuing their unique ways of communicating.'
> (Blank and Bevan, 2017)

Babies pick up on and begin to interpret your facial expressions as well as the tone of your voice and expression very early on. For all babies, regardless of the languages they are exposed to, using animated facial expressions and an expressive and excited tone of voice is appropriate when the baby is alert, whereas a more relaxed face and a calmer voice is more appropriate at nap time or during feeding time.

It comes quite naturally to many people to speak in really simple language rather than long full sentences when communicating with babies. Babies start to understand words for the most important people and things in their life, such as 'mummy', 'daddy', 'milk', 'teddy' when they hear these words regularly.

If all adults in the baby's life are responsive to the child and communicating with them as described above, they are in a good position to pick up more than one language if both languages are spoken to them in this way.

Interacting with children aged 18 months – 3 years

Some children are introduced to a new language while they are in the early stages of learning their first language. These children will still be learning their first language. In order for these children to learn both languages, they must hear regular good language models in each language. The section below about supporting sequential learners contains lot of practical advice and tips that are also appropriate for many children under the age of 3 years. Keeping the six principles for good quality adult-child interaction in mind will support you to interact with these children in the appropriate way.

Interacting with children who are new to English (sequential learners)

The way you interact with a child will depend on how much English they have picked up. Your interactions with a child will change as they learn more and more English as the weeks and months pass. You therefore need to continue to observe and reflect on the child's abilities, and alter the way you are interacting accordingly.

Below is a range of key strategies to use when interacting with children who are new to English. These strategies support children to develop their understanding of English and also to develop their use of English once they start to experiment with this new language.

Chapter Five Adult-Child Interaction

language they hear you say will be more meaningful to them, making it more likely that they will retain this new vocabulary.

As adults we naturally ask each other many questions, however when a child has very limited skills in a new language, asking them questions like 'what is that for?', 'what are you going to do next?', 'what colour is that?' actually puts pressure on a child and can be a cause of stress if they do not have the language skills to answer the questions that you are asking. Children also often feel like they are being tested, which can actually make them reluctant to respond and can take the fun out of communication.

Elks and McLachlan (2016) recommend making four comments for every question that you ask a child. For example, if you ask the child 'which colour would you like?', you may follow this up with comments such as 'ooh orange', 'that's a nice colour', 'great painting', 'wow, a flower!'. For children who are very new to English, consider making at least five or six comments for every question that you ask. This

- ### Comment more, question less
  Comment on what the child is doing or what they are looking at. For example, if the child is building a tower you could make comments like 'you're building', 'wow... it's a big tower', '1, 2, 3... oh crash'. If they are washing their hands you might make comments like 'wash, wash, wash', 'rub, rub, rub', 'ooh lovely clean hands!' If a group of children are hopping from one end of the outdoor play area to the other, you could say 'you're hopping', 'hop, hop, hop', 'good hopping'. In this situation, the repetition of the word 'hop' whilst the children are actually hopping will help the children to link the word 'hop' to the action, helping them to build their English vocabulary.

  For children who are in the early stages of learning a new language, hearing comments like the examples above is actually far more valuable than being asked questions. This is because hearing comments that relate to what the child is doing or seeing, actually teaches the children words in their new language and enables them to make links. When a child is having fun and doing an activity of interest to them, the

Chapter Five Adult-Child Interaction

will provide them with models of language without putting pressure on them to use the new language before they are ready.

- **Use simple language**
  Try to keep your language simple and use short phrases rather than long complicated ones. You can usually tell if a child has understood what you have said based on their reaction, so respond to the child. If you can tell that they have not understood, simplify what you have said and make more use of non-verbal communication or visuals for example. You can also emphasise key words to help the children understand what you're saying.

- **Use lots of non-verbal communication to help the child understand what you say**
  Non-verbal communication (e.g. gestures and facial expressions) is incredibly powerful. When requesting that the children put their coats on, miming putting on a coat or pointing to the child's coat whilst making the request makes it much easier for the child to understand. Many practitioners naturally do this when interacting with toddlers and young children.

- **Use other visuals to support the child to understand what you're saying**
  Pictures and photographs are so powerful when there is a language barrier. They actually show the child what you mean when you are not able to successfully get a message across using words. For example, if you're going to walk to the local library, you can show them where you are going beforehand using a picture of the library from the internet. Similarly, if it is time for assembly, you can show them a picture that you have previously taken of the children sitting in the hall for assembly, to help them understand where you are going.

- **Talk about 'the here and now'**
  Children will find it easier to understand what is being said if you're talking about things that are happening at the time, and things that they can see. They may find it very difficult to understand what you are saying if you are talking about something that will be happening next week or next month for example.

- **Enjoy music and songs together!**
  Musical activities are incredibly valuable for promoting additional language learning. Songs with actions are

usually very popular with children and they also give children who are completely new to English a way to join in.

'Simple songs, rhymes and refrains chanted in a rhythmic way are often the vehicle for children's first attempts to articulate an additional language.' (Drury and Robertson, 2008)

- **Praise the child regularly to boost their confidence and self-esteem**
  This is vital as children need to be confident in the setting in order to make attempts at using new words in a new language.

- **Respond to the child's non-verbal communication**
  Children with limited English will rely heavily on non-verbal communication when they first enter your setting. A child may point to the garden, or fetch their coat to indicate that they would like to go outside, or take your hand to go to the toilet. This is a good time to model words to the child, such as 'let's go outside'.

Chapter Five Adult-Child Interaction

You will be able to gain a lot of information about how the child might be feeling by looking at their facial expressions and body language, so tune in to their non-verbal communication and respond to that in a warm, caring manner.

- **Make the most of everyday situations**

  'There must be frequent and meaningful episodes of interaction with others. All activities, such as putting on a coat or having a piece of fruit, provide opportunities for conceptual development and they must be accompanied by the practitioners' use of language.' (Drury and Robertson, 2008)

- **Promote interactions with peers without pressuring the children**

  You can support the children with their social communication skills during almost any activity, for example, when outside, model cooperative play such as throwing a ball back and forth with someone. Children learn so much English through playing together as they have fun, chat, negotiate rules and disagree! Even if they are playing silently but communicating using non-verbal communication, this is a great process for a child who is new in an unfamiliar language environment.

  For those who find it a bit more difficult to get involved with other children, 'gradually help them to make small steps towards joining the play, using information gained from home about what they enjoy.' (Blank and Bevan, 2017)

- **Give the child time**

  When you talk to a child, they need time to process and try and make sense of what you have said and then to come up with a response. Elks and McLachlan (2016) suggest that adults should give children 10 seconds to respond. For children who are new to English, it is very important that you give them this time.

- **Model language in a positive way, rather than correcting a child's language**

  If a child uses the wrong word for something, or they say something that isn't grammatically correct for example, you can model the correct way or saying it in a positive way. For example, if a child says 'look, two mouses!', you could say 'oh yes, two little mice!' This way you're allowing the child to hear correct models of spoken language whilst actually praising and encouraging the child's efforts at the same time.

- **Join in with the child's play and follow their lead**

  For example, if a child is enjoying pushing a train around the train track, pick up a train and join in with this. Use simple language to talk about what the child is doing and what the child can see. Make lots of symbolic noises, such as 'choo choo' or animal noises if playing with animals, as often children join in with these noises. This can be a great way of developing their confidence to use their voice more in this new setting.

- **Be aware of the speed of your speech**

  Speak in a natural way but make a conscious effort not to speak too quickly. Due to our busy lives, many of us have a habit of speaking very quickly.

- **Use a sign-support system such as Signalong or Makaton**

  Using signs whilst talking can make it easier for children to understand what you are saying.

Chapter Five Adult-Child Interaction

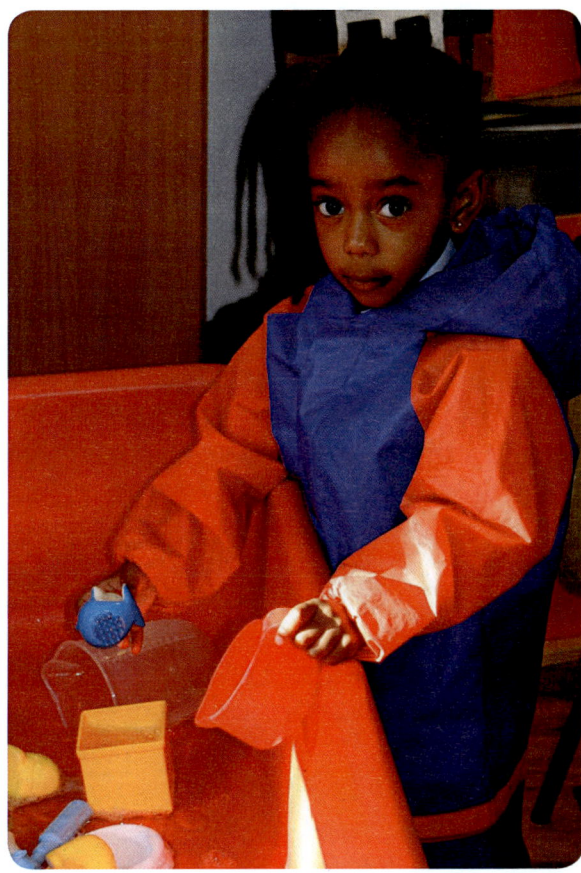

Interacting with a child during the 'silent period'

The way you as practitioners interact with EAL learners who are going through a silent period is really important because it will impact on how they feel, as well as the English that they learn. We want to enable them to feel comfortable enough and confident enough to have a go at communicating using their voice when they feel ready to do so.

- At this stage in their development **children need time to quietly absorb the language** around them. Ensure that you are offering a supportive, pressure-free environment with good models of language for the child to hear because during the silent period, children are taking in an awful lot and constantly learning about the new language.

- When the child communicates non-verbally (e.g. using pointing or nodding their head), **respond positively** to this communication. For example, if the child points to the fruit that they would like rather than naming it, accept this response and give them the fruit that they have requested non-verbally.

- Play games and **activities that don't require a verbal response**, such as scavenger hunts, musical statues, sleeping lions, Simon says and assault courses and ensure that the child experiences success in these activities.

- During other planned activities, **make sure there are ways that the child can respond without needing to talk** so as not to put pressure on a child to speak. For example, you might have a 'choice board' that the child can use when it is their turn to choose a nursery rhyme for the group to sing. Registration could involve self-registration on a board or the child could indicate that they are present during the register by raising their hand or nodding their head.

- **Be responsive** to any attempts the child makes to communicate. It might not always be obvious that the child is trying to communicate with you, so look out for signs and subtle changes in their facial expressions and body language that may indicate that they want to communicate a message.

- **Sing songs that have actions** as children can join in using the actions, without being pressured to use the words.

- **Give these children plenty of positive reinforcement** when they play with others, complete tasks or try new things, for example. We want them to feel confident enough to attempt to use English when they feel they are ready to try.

Providing opportunities for children to use their home language (EAL requirement 1)

Continuing to improve their skills in their home language will make it easier for a child to learn an additional language, so in order to support the learning of English, it is also essential to continue to support the development of the child's home language.

'For a child who has limited understanding of English, opportunities to use their home language can be like turning on a light in a dark room; the setting and all its possibilities are opened up.' (Primary National Strategy, 2007)

Chapter Five Adult-Child Interaction

How you give the child opportunities to use their home language in your setting will depend on whether or not there is anyone in the setting who shares the same home language as the child.

If you have other children in the setting who speak the same language there are endless opportunities to facilitate activities and opportunities for them to use their home language together to carry out tasks and activities; use your imagination and get creative!

If you have a staff member who is able to speak the child's home language it is easy to create opportunities for them to use and develop their home language.

The adult can join in with the child at various times throughout the day, during a range of different types of activities.

If they work in a different room, perhaps they could join the child at snack times and lunchtimes for example.

Develop their skills in their home language in the following ways:

- **Add to what the child has said** in his or her home language. For example, if the child says 'juice all gone' in their home language, the adult could say 'yes juice is all gone…your cup is empty', also in the child's home language. Hearing you extend their speech shows the child how they can create longer sentences.

- Speak with the child **using language that is just slightly ahead** of the language that they are using. This will support the child to develop his or her home language.

- **Introduce any new concepts in the child's home language**. For example, if exposing the child to materials of unusual textures, use new words such as 'rough' or 'spikey' in the child's home language first.

- Provide **activities that allow them to make discoveries** to enable them to extend their thinking and talk together about the discoveries that they have made.

If there are no staff members in the setting who speak the child's home language, it is of course more of a challenge to provide opportunities for the child to use and develop their home language. It is nevertheless an absolute priority. As well as learning and using some key words and phrases in the child's home language, practitioners should find ways to give their key children opportunities for play and learning in their first language.

Below are some examples of ways to provide opportunities for the child to use and develop their home language, even if no adults in your setting share the child's home language:

- Having such easy **access to the internet** is very useful! Episodes of children's programmes are available in different languages online. Similarly, there are many interactive online materials and educational games that can support with each child's development of their home language. For example:
  - https://www.bbc.co.uk/cbeebies/lingoshow
  - http://www.bbc.co.uk/schools/websites/4_11/site/languages.shtml

Chapter Five Adult-Child Interaction

- Consider whether parents or other family members can be invited into your setting for some activities or events to facilitate development in the child's home language. See page 66 to see how one setting holds annual events which promote the development of each child's first language.

- **Dual-language books** are fantastic resources. They can be used with a whole group or on a 1:1 basis or with a small group of children. For a younger child in your setting, you might be looking at the pictures together and naming items in the child's home language as well as in English.

  For slightly older children, it can also be a great idea to make recordings of someone reading the book in the child's home language. Listening stations can then be used to enable several children to each listen to a story in their home language at the same time. You could ask parents or carers to record themselves reading a story in their home language, if they are willing. You can use any recording device that you are able to lend to parents.

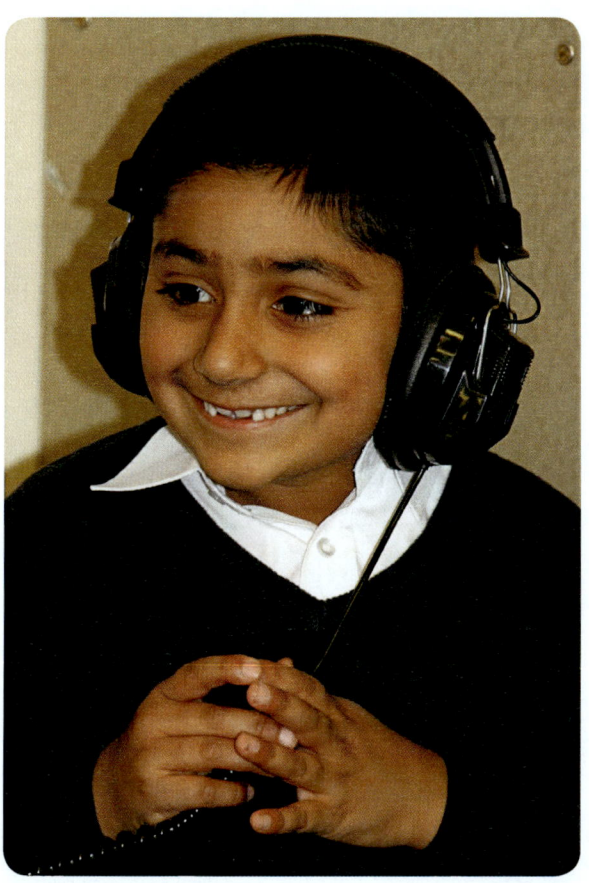

  It can also be useful to send books home for parents and children to look at and read together in their home language. They will then be familiar with the story so that when it is then read in English in your setting, the child will have an understanding of what is happening and they may be able to pick up some English vocabulary while listening. (Sargent, 2016)

- **Voice recording devices** and dual-listening stations can be used in many other ways to allow all children to hear the same piece of information in their home language. You could do this to introduce a new topic or prepare the children for a one off activity or event such as sports day. This of course takes some forward planning as you would need to ask a parent or carer or someone else to make the recording for you.

- If you have several children who all speak the same language, consider the possibility of having a **parent volunteer coming in regularly to read a story** to the whole group (or a smaller group) of children in their home language. Children who don't speak this language will also benefit from this experience. It will help them to develop an understanding of the existence of other languages and to develop empathy for their peers. You could ask the children who are not familiar with the language being spoken if they can guess how to say certain words in this unfamiliar language. For example, if reading 'Dear Zoo' in Polish, can the children who do not speak Polish guess what the word is for 'elephant'? Due to the repetitive nature of many children's books, children are often able to identify what words mean in different languages when hearing them over and over again.

- **Singing songs and nursery rhymes together** is a great way of sharing languages and cultures.

  Can children or parents teach you some simple songs or nursery rhymes in their home language? They may be able to translate common children's songs and rhymes (e.g. The wheels on the bus, Twinkle, twinkle, little star) or they may be able to teach you traditional songs in their own language. Songs and rhymes can support language learning as they are often repetitive and the actions that accompany the words in many songs help to reinforce the meaning.

Chapter Five Adult-Child Interaction

and importantly when children are playing with each other. So your role as a practitioner is to interact with children through play as well as to facilitate and promote play between peers, in a non-pressured manner.

> *'Play cannot be wrong. It therefore provides a safe situation for the child to try out new things without the fear of failure. This is important for the child's development of a positive self-esteem.'* (Beaver et al., 2002)

Cultural differences in play

It is important to be aware that there are differences between cultures in attitudes towards play. The way in which children play, and adults do and do not interact with children through play, varies greatly from culture to culture. Similarly, attitudes towards the value of play are also different.

Roopnarine (2010) found that 'parents in western, technologically developed societies were more likely to embrace play as important for children's cognitive

Many songs and rhymes can be found in different languages on the internet. For example, there are 'hello songs', 'counting songs' and many other songs in a range of languages at www.bbc.co.uk/cbeebies/shows/lingo-show.

- Have fun when playing together!

The importance of play

> *'Play is essential for children's development, building their confidence as they learn to explore, to think about problems, and relate to others.'* (EYFS, 2017)

Play not only helps children to develop language skills in their home language, it also plays a vital role in supporting children to learn a new language. (Beaver et al., 2002) This is because relaxed and enjoyable play situations give children the chance to practise and consolidate new skills in a fun and familiar way. They will be able to try out new words when they are ready, whilst learning new things and making discoveries. This refers to when adults and children are playing together

Chapter Five Adult-Child Interaction

offer EAL language programmes that are specifically designed to help children learn English. Ideally, the staff member running the groups should be able to speak the home language of the children in the group. This often works particularly well in settings that cater for large numbers of children who speak the same language, however it is more challenging when there are only one or two children speaking each language in the setting.

The case study below shows how one setting runs EAL groups for EYFS children.

and social development and to see themselves as play partners to children'. In more traditional non-western societies, parents often do not consider play to be of great importance, they simply think of play as something that children just do.

Due to cultural differences, some children may not be used to having an adult join them in play, and at first they may feel uncomfortable or confused by this. Be aware that it may take time for a child to become familiar and comfortable with this new learning environment. (Blank and Bevan, 2017)

Explain to parents that children find out about their world and learn many new skills during play. In addition, 'through play, children develop physical, intellectual, linguistic, social and emotional skills and concepts.' (Beaver et al., 2002)

EAL language programmes

In order to ensure that all children have the opportunity to reach a good standard of English, some settings

Case Study: EAL language programmes

This setting, located in Greater London caters for a high number of EAL learners, therefore EAL language groups are delivered by a staff member who is employed specifically to run this intervention.

The EAL learners in the EYFS attend a 30 minute group session on a daily basis (5 days per week) for a block of 6 weeks at a time. Groups typically contain 4-5 EAL learners.

Each child's abilities in a range of language and communication skills are rated before and after the 6-week block. Skills being rated include the child's ability to make greetings in English and the child's confidence levels in interacting with other children in the setting.

Every session starts with a hello song and a greetings activity. Puppets are used to introduce a new topic every week. Topics include 'ourselves', 'animals' and 'food'. Each session finishes with a turn-taking game and a goodbye song.

Staff have reported that the outcomes are typically very good and the majority of children make progress in all of the areas being assessed.

Chapter Six Building positive relationships with parents and carers

'Settings need to build partnerships with families of EAL children, in order for children to achieve.'
(Brodie and Savage, 2015)

Developing a positive relationship with the parents or carers of all children in your setting is fundamental in helping the children to thrive and develop as best they can.

For children who are learning English as an additional language, it is hugely important to have good communication between staff and parents so that each child's unique language needs are understood along with their levels of learning and development.

Chapter three (helping children to settle-in) covered the initial information sharing meeting (see pages 31-35), which is an opportunity to start building a rapport with a child's parents and to gain their trust. This chapter looks further at how to build on that initial relationship.

This chapter also discusses potential challenges with developing parent relationships and explores ways to overcome these challenges if they occur. It also explores how to work in partnership and build a relationship with parents who speak very little or no English, with advice on how to work with interpreters. A number of perspectives of parents are also included in this chapter.

Chapter Six Building positive relationships with parents and carers

What does the EYFS say?

The EYFS seeks to provide: 'partnership working between practitioners and with parents and/or carers' (EYFS, 2017).

Developing partnership working with parents

'The benefit to young children and their families of positive, mutually respectful relationships between parents and early years practitioners has been evidenced through research studies carried out over a number of years.' (Brunton and Thornton, 2010)

The benefits of good partnership working:

- The child will see this positive relationship and this will act as a model of relationships for the child.
- Concerns shared can be monitored or acted upon as appropriate.

- Parents will be clear about what is happening and when.
- It helps parents to feel reassured about the quality of care that their child is receiving.
- If any issues arise it will be easier to discuss and address these.
- The parent is more likely to follow through with any recommendations if they have a good relationship with the person giving the advice.

What does a good relationship between a parent and a practitioner look like?

- The parent finds the practitioner approachable.
- The practitioner is genuinely warm, friendly and welcoming.
- Both the practitioner and parent listen to one other.
- Both the parent and the practitioner share important information relating to the child with one another. For example, as well as sharing information about everyday life such as eating and toileting routines, you might tell the parent of an EAL learner if their child joined in with a song for the first time, or if they made their first attempts to speak in English. As a result, the parents feel informed about how their child is doing within the setting.

General advice to promote good relationship building

Remember that 'all parents want the best for their own learners.' (Sood and Mistry, 2015) If they can see that you too want the best for their child they are likely to engage in a relationship with you for the good of their child.

In your role as a key person, it is important to do all of the following in order to develop good partnerships with parents:

- **'Treat the parent as a person in their own right**, asking how they are and making good use of verbal and non-verbal communication.' (Soni, 2013) Smile and greet parents and children in a friendly manner whenever you see them.

- **Have regular discussions with the parents** so that they feel included and 'in the know' about what their child has been up to. These don't need to be long discussions. There are plenty of ideas about how to do this with parents who have limited abilities in English later in this chapter on page 67.

Chapter Six Building positive relationships with parents and carers

- **Make parents feel as though they and their family are valued.** Recognise, share and talk in a positive way about the religious and cultural events that those in your setting are celebrating. For example, Eid, Chinese New Year, Hanukah, Diwali and Easter. The more accepted and valued parents feel, the better the chances are that they will feel comfortable with you and form a good working relationship.

- **Share photographs with parents.** If there is one thing that all parents love, it is seeing photographs and video clips of things that their child has done when they were not there to witness it first-hand. Seeing these photos and videos often makes parents feel more included and informed about their child's nursery experience. This whole sharing experience can help to build trust and really strengthen relationships between practitioners and parents.

Some settings use secure online platforms that allow parents to log-in to see pictures of their child. Some settings also post pictures of children on their website, with previous consent from parents of course.

- **Hold regular events and celebrations and invite parents.** For example, you might have regular 'stay and play' sessions or a range of annual events such as a summer picnic, a sports day or even charity events such as bake sales.

This setting in Greater London hold an annual event for 'World Book Day' where parents are invited to stay and look at books together with their children.

Case Study: Annual events

In this setting based in Greater London, the EYFS holds a number of annual events that parents and carers are invited to. As well as being incredibly exciting for the children, these events promote learning and development in many areas and they also support partnership working and relationship building with parents.

World Book Day
Every March, on World Book Day, children are invited to dress up in a costume from home (or from the selection of fancy dress items in the setting) and bring in a book from home to share. Parents can stay and look at their own books with their children and also look at the books in the setting. The selection of dual-language books is always put out for speakers of other languages to enjoy.

World food event
Every summer, parents are invited to attend with their children and sample the foods on offer at the school's world food event. Staff members cook a variety of foods from their country of origin, or a country that interests them. Some parents also cook foods from their home culture.

Cultural differences are celebrated and many photographs are taken, which are then displayed on the nursery's photo wall.

Chapter Six Building positive relationships with parents and carers

- **Be accepting of cultural differences and individual circumstances.**

Some parents naturally worry more than others, some have more questions than others, and some parents will have more confidence than others. Many parents will be seeking reassurance from you about their child's progress with settling-in and communication development.

Some families may be dealing with a whole host of challenging circumstances such as debt, illness of a close relative, grief, mental health problems. As a result of personal circumstances, it may take longer to build a relationship with some parents than others.

There are many factors that can also impact on opportunities for communication. These include: 'post-natal depression, economic stress, illness, ack of confidence, low expectations, differing cultural influences.
(Desforges and Abouchaar, 2003 in Elks and McLachlan, 2016)

Potential challenges to partnership working

It may be particularly challenging to develop a good relationship with parents of EAL learners if any of the following circumstances apply:

- The child's parents have very little or no English and no adults in the setting speak a language in common with them.
- The child is regularly dropped off at the setting by someone other than a parent.
- The child has poor attendance with long periods of absence.
- The parent does not engage in conversations.
- The parent has experience of a very different type of early years setting where partnership working is not expected or encouraged (or the parent hasn't had any previous experience of school or education themselves).
- The parent has mental health problems.
- There are safeguarding concerns and the child is on a child in need plan or a child protection plan.
- The family are asylum seekers or refugees who have recently moved to the country.

In some cases, more than one of the circumstances above may apply which may make partnership working even more challenging. However, most practitioners manage to develop very positive relationships with many parents who fall into one or more of the above categories.

Overcoming potential challenges

If the parent has very limited or no English, try the following:

- If there are no adults in your setting who speak a language in common with the parents, **you will need to use interpreters to communicate effectively**. Some parents will have a friend or a relative who is able to translate for them. Alternatively, there may be another parent who can help to interpret information. This should be done with great caution, as it could be uncomfortable for some families if discussions are around personal circumstances, for example.

If you require access to an interpreter and you do not currently have access to one, it is advised that you contact your local education authority who should be able to direct or advise you. In some areas, telephone interpreting services exist. These can be particularly useful, as you can call them at any time of the day and request an interpreter of any language when an unexpected situation occurs and an interpreter has not been pre-booked.

On page 72 there is some useful information about how best to make use of interpreters.

- You will also need to '**provide written materials in the family's native language** whenever possible.' (asha.org)

- **Regularly show parents photographs or videos** of their child. This way you can show parents what the child has done in the setting without having to rely on language. Make an extra effort to do this more with parents who don't speak English so that they feel more informed and involved with what the child is doing from day-to-day.

- If the parent is interested in learning English, **can you recommend any English classes** that parents could

Chapter Six Building positive relationships with parents and carers

attend? You may know of a local adult education centre that is offering English courses, for example, or your setting might be offering something more informal such as a coffee morning where a few key words in English are taught each week.

If a child is always dropped off and collected by someone else, try the following:

- **Sending messages through other people**. This can be effective in some cases, however often messages can get lost in translation or simply forgotten. In addition, you would not want to be raising some issues with someone other than a parent.

- **Set up a communication book** that the child brings to the setting every day and takes home again at the end of every day. Information can be written in here by practitioners to parents and of course parents can write messages to the practitioners. However if you are communicating with parents through communication books, be aware of the literacy abilities of parents, as some parents may have difficulties with reading and writing.

- **Liaising by email** can be a great way to keep in regular contact if the parent has good enough literacy skills as well as easy access to the internet.

- **Consider arranging a weekly or fortnightly phone call** with a parent if they will not be bringing or dropping off their child in the long-term. This does not need to be a lengthy call, it is simply to touch base, clarify any important information, raise any concerns or issues and to keep the positive relationship that it is so necessary to build and maintain.

If the child has poor attendance with long periods of absence, try the following:

- **Identify the reason** for lengthy absences and think about whether or not there is anything you can do as a setting to help. A staff member with a positive relationship with the parent should address this in a supportive manner. Possible reasons for lengthy periods of absence include: illness, family circumstances and lengthy visits to their country of origin.

- Continue to **adopt a no-blame culture** and be as supportive and non-judgemental as possible. From the term after a child's fifth birthday they are legally required to attend a setting, however before this point, there is no legal requirement.

If the parent does not engage in conversations, try the following:

- **Consider potential reasons why** the parent might not be engaging in conversations with you. This could be due to a whole host of reasons, including cultural differences in relation to making small talk, a lack of confidence or difficulties using English. If you are able to identify the underlying reason, this will enable you to provide additional and appropriate support if necessary.

- **Persevere** and continue to make an effort with the parent. Do not let the fact that a parent may not be communicative stop you from making an effort with them. Many parents need to gain your trust before they will be happy to communicate naturally with you.

- Remember **everyone is different**. Some people are much more forthcoming from the outset, whereas others need a bit of time before they will converse.

- **Think about your body language** and the messages that you are conveying through this. Perhaps ask others in your setting if your approach is friendly and welcoming.

- **Consider other ways to communicate** if necessary. Some parents might find it easier to communicate with you in a different way. Perhaps try a home-to-setting communication book or discuss the option of emailing parents if this is appropriate.

If the parent has experience of a very different type of early years setting where partnership working is not expected or encouraged, try the following:

- Ensure that in your initial parent meeting, you have clearly explained the nature of the early years setting and the importance of partnership working.

- Arrange an additional meeting if necessary to ensure that they understand the ins and outs of how early years settings work in this country.

Chapter Six Building positive relationships with parents and carers

- 'Stay and play' sessions can be very beneficial for both relationship building with parents as well as promoting and demonstrating approaches to play.

- These strategies are also useful when developing relationships with parents who have not had any previous experience of school or education themselves.

If the parent has mental health problems, try the following:

- **Be as understanding** and as supportive as possible. Telling others about a personal mental health difficulty is not an easy task for a parent. In many cases, the parent will not share with you the fact that they have mental health difficulties.

- Some early years settings have access to a **family support worker**, for example many nurseries that are part of mainstream primary schools. In some situations, putting parents in contact with people in these roles can be really beneficial to both the parent and the children.

- **Always consider the safety of the child** and be sure to follow the setting's safeguarding and welfare policy if you have concerns about their safety or well-being.

If there are any safeguarding concerns and the child is on a child in need plan or a child protection plan, try the following:

- **Be honest with parents**. In order to develop a good relationship parents need to develop trust in you.

- Make sure you and all other staff members are very **familiar with your setting's safeguarding policies and procedures** and be sure to follow these.

If the family are asylum seekers or refugees who have recently moved to the country, try the following:

- Be aware that **building or developing a relationship with some parents from an asylum seeker or refugee background can take longer than you expect**.

Depending on the family's situation, they may have other priorities such as for example, dealing with poor quality housing, being separated from other family members, or appealing a decision regarding their immigration status. Also, if parents know that it is likely that they will be relocating again in the near future, they may not be motivated to put effort into relationship building.

- The approaches you take will depend on the situation and the family's circumstances.

- 'All staff need to be aware of and sensitive to the potential difficulties new arrivals and their families may be experiencing.' (New Arrival Excellence Programme Guidance, 2007)

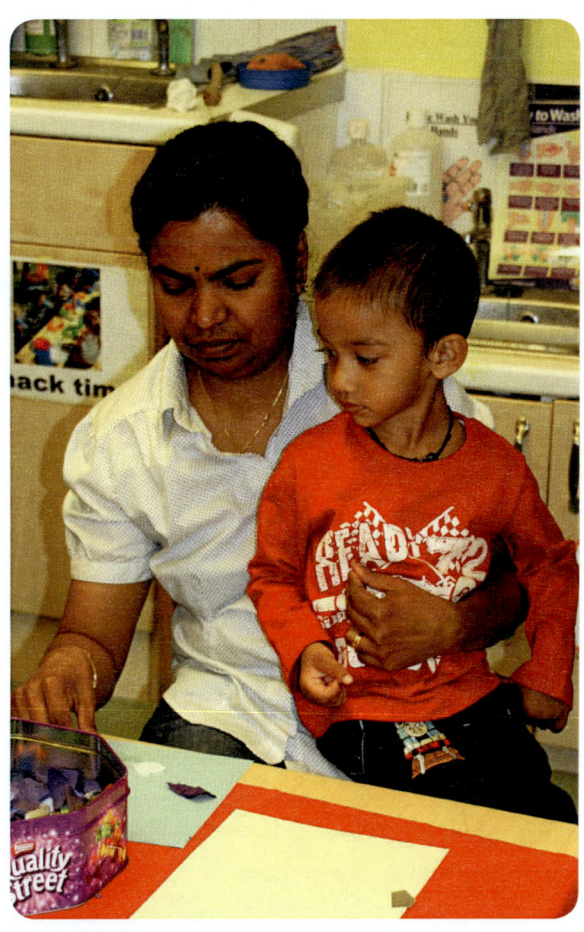

Chapter Six Building positive relationships with parents and carers

Key messages to give to parents

Parents often have questions about the impact that learning more than one language can have on their child and it is important to give them the following key messages:

- **Bilingualism is an advantage**

  'Children learning EAL have the potential to become high-achieving and successful lifelong learners.' (Sargent, 2016)

  There are **many benefits and advantages to learning more than one language**. Rodriguez (2014) draws together research about the benefits of learning more than one language. She reports that advantages of bilingualism relate to '**metalinguistic awareness, cognitive development, academic achievement, and cross-cultural awareness and understanding.**'

- **It is important that children continue to develop their skills in their home language.**

Explain to parents that it is important that they continue to speak their home language with their child. Refer to pages 15 and 16 for more information about why the child's home language is of such great importance.

General advice to give to parents about supporting language development at home (EAL Requirement 2).

Some parents will be knowledgeable and skilled in supporting their child's language development at home, however many parents benefit from some guidance from practitioners. Research carried out by the National Literacy Trust in 2011 found that many parents don't recognise the importance of communicating with their baby or toddler, so the guidance you give to parents about interaction is crucial.

It is recommended that parents do the following:

- **Talk with their child** during everyday activities (e.g. when walking to nursery, point out buses and birds, or when getting ready for nursery, name body parts and items of clothing together).

- **Add to what their child says**. For example, if the child says 'qen' (which means 'dog' in Albanian), the parent could say 'quen I madh' (which means 'big dog' in Albanian).

- **Try to have tech-free times** when together, with no TV on and no tablet or phone out.

- **Have fun playing together** with their child. Be aware that attitudes towards play and behaviours vary greatly between cultures. 'Families have different styles and engagement with play at home and may not necessarily view play as a time to interact and develop language skills.' (Elks and McLachlan, 2016) See pages 62-63 for information about cultural difference in relation to play.

- **Limit the amount of time their child spends watching TV** or playing on computer games or tablets. Although the programmes that children watch often have good models of language, children who spend a large amount of their waking hours watching TV or playing on a handheld device have

Chapter Six Building positive relationships with parents and carers

limited opportunities to develop their language and communication skills. Children need continuous interaction with others in order to develop their language and communication. (Gibbons, 1991)

- Read, sing nursery rhymes, visit the library, and explore outdoor spaces together.

- **Home Activity Sheets**

Consider giving out a 'home activity sheet' to parents each week (or every couple of weeks) with ideas about games and activities that they can do at home or when out and about with their child. Examples of activities include scavenger hunts and games such as 'Simon says'.

Suggest that parents set aside time each week to have a go at the activities on the sheet and of course advise parents to do these activities and games in their home language. This is a great way to support their child's language development at home.

Be sure to touch base with them after giving out activity sheets to see if they manage to do the activities and to see how they went. This weekly chat about how the activities went at home is also a fantastic way to ensure that you continue to build positive relationships with parents.

See pages 96-102 in the resources section for a range of 'home activity sheet' ideas as well as a blank template for you to use.

Practitioner perspective

"We've found that since we've given the parents little activities to do at home each week, many of them have been much more engaged as they want to tell us how the activities went. Of course, not everyone does the activities but in general the parents are keen to give them a try. The children also love talking to each other about what they have done at home."

Chapter Six Building positive relationships with parents and carers

Case Study: Parental concerns

Child's name: Filip
Age: 4 years, 2 months
Home language: Polish
Background information: Filip was born in the UK. Both of his parents are Polish speakers, however Filip's father is very proficient in English. Filip's mother currently has a basic level of English. She is attending English language classes and is improving her English skills on a daily basis.

Filip's mum wondered if she should stop speaking Polish to Filip at home, to help him learn English. She told Filip's key person that that she didn't want him to be behind the other children in English.

Filip's key person explained the importance of continuing to speak Polish. She explained how important it is for Filip to continue to improve his skills in Polish to support his learning and cognitive development. She told Filip's mum that the better he is at Polish, the easier it will be for him to learn English.

Filip's key person also explained that good skills in Filip's first language are very important to keep his family connections, for example when speaking to grandparents or other members of the family.

Working with interpreters

Having a conversation or meeting with a parent using an interpreter can feel a little daunting initially. However once you have used an interpreter a couple of times, it soon begins to feel much more natural.

Below is some advice for working with interpreters:

Speak to the interpreter before the meeting.
It is helpful to have a conversation with the interpreter prior to the meeting (i.e. without the parents present) to briefly outline the purpose of the meeting and the topics to be discussed, etc.

Allow more time for a meeting if you will be using an interpreter.
Meetings can often take twice as long when using interpreters so make allowances for this.

Speak to the parent rather than to the interpreter.
It can be tempting to speak to the interpreter rather than to the parent, however in order to develop a positive relationship and make the parent feel valued, make a conscious effort to talk directly to the parent.

Make sure you pause.
Be sure to give the interpreter enough time to think about how to translate something. Often, some things that we say are not easily translated, so an interpreter might need longer to interpret them.

Try to use relatively short, concise sentences when possible.
This is important because the interpreter has to remember what you have said and translate it into the parent's language. It will be harder for them to translate accurately if you have used long sentences.

If possible, try and **use the same interpreter for future meetings.**
This is reassuring and comforting for the parent, and the interpreter will have some background knowledge of the family and the situation.

(http://www.asha.org/practice/multicultural/issues/interpret.htm)

Practitioner perspective

"Before using an interpreter, I was quite nervous. However, once we got started it was all fine. My manager gave me a few tips about using interpreters, for example making sure that I spoke to the parent and not to the interpreter. I feel like I have a better relationship with the parent now and it was great because the parent could explain themselves properly."

Chapter Seven
Observation, assessment and planning

Observing children as they play and interact and using this information to guide your planning is a crucial part of the whole early years process of helping young children to learn and develop.

Featherstone (2013) explains that 'when children learn, they are constantly restructuring the connections between brain cells, making new links, reinforcing old ones, and pruning those that have ceased to be relevant. This process is both fascinating to watch and extremely difficult to capture, particularly in the early years when the brain-building is at its most complex and rapid.'

As children develop so quickly in the first five years of their lives, it is important that observation, assessment and planning are an ongoing and continuous cycle. It is also key that all staff members feed into this cycle and share their observations in an effective way.

For children learning EAL, the observation, assessment and planning cycle is equally significant in helping them to make progress. The difference for these children is that a greater emphasis is placed on certain aspects of their development while they are adjusting to a new language environment and learning this new language.

This chapter highlights the importance of nurturing the personal, social and emotional development of children who are being exposed to English for the first time when entering the setting.

Chapter Seven Observation, assessment and planning

The Prime Areas of Learning and Development

Communication and Language	Personal, Social and Emotional Development (PSED)	Physical Development
Listening and Attention	Self-Confidence and Self-Awareness	Moving and Handling
Understanding	Managing Feelings and Behaviour	Health and Self-Care
Speaking	Making Relationships	

The prime areas of communication and language and PSED are very interlinked. For all children, in order to progress in communication and language, they need to have the self-confidence to interact with peers and to develop relationships. For those learning EAL, personal, social and emotional development is key; a child's overall well-being plays a huge part in how easy it will be for them to develop skills in a new language.

Depending on how each child settles into your setting, a different amount of emphasis may be placed on particular areas within the prime area of PSED; some children will need more support managing their feelings or developing self-confidence, for example. It is important to nurture these qualities early on so that once a child is confident to interact with others in their new surroundings, further development can flourish. The child's emotional development is a priority as their language will only progress when they are comfortable and feeling secure and happy in the setting.

The importance of communication and language and PSED does in no way diminish the importance of the child's physical development.

You may find that a child who is silent gains great confidence from physical achievements and finds social interaction more natural as they play alongside others on equipment. Physical activities are an excellent medium for supporting understanding, for example, through following rules, and hearing action words such as 'run', 'stop', 'hide', 'count' etc. It is therefore a good idea to use physical activities as a motivator for learning language and developing social interaction.

The key characteristics of effective early learning

As well as your ongoing observations around the areas of learning and development and the aspects within them, you must also notice 'how' children learn, by using the EYFS 'three key characteristics of effective early learning'.

To notice 'how' children learn, enables you as a practitioner not only to gather information around children's abilities to explore, concentrate and work things out, but to find out what they get excited about, what fires their enthusiasm and what captures their focused attention. That is when you find out what they can do!

Chapter Seven Observation, assessment and planning

different learning style (e.g. some children may be from cultures that do not encourage play). For these reasons, the way these children learn may change over time, as they adapt and get used to the learning environment.

Continuous observation and reflection is key here as 'practitioners can't rely on the child telling them in English about what they enjoy or what motivates them or to talk about their thinking. It may relate to taking time to watch, listen and think about what is happening to find patterns in what helps a child learn effectively.' (Soni, 2013)

It is reported that the abilities of EAL learners is often underestimated (Primary National Strategy, 2011), which can result in these children often achieving poor outcomes at the end of the EYFS. For these very reasons, identifying the learning style and exactly 'how' each EAL child learns is crucial in order for them to make progress and to achieve outcomes that truly reflect their abilities in each of the areas of learning and development at the end of the EYFS.

Three key characteristics of effective learning:

- '**playing and exploring** – children investigate and experience things and 'have a go'

- **active learning** – children concentrate and keep on trying if they encounter difficulties, and enjoy achievements

- **creating and thinking critically** – children have and develop their own ideas, make links between ideas, and develop strategies for doing things.'

(EYFS, 2017)

When considering how each child learns in relation to these three key characteristics of effective learning, remember that learners of EAL may or may not be used to the types of resources and materials that you have in your setting. Similarly, they may be used to a very

Chapter Seven Observation, assessment and planning

What is observation?
- Observation involves 'reaching an understanding of children's learning by **watching, listening to, and interacting with children as they engage in activities and experiences** and demonstrate their specific knowledge, skills and understanding.' (DfE, 2012)

What is assessment?
- Dubiel (2016) highlights that 'there exists a profound and widespread misunderstanding of what assessment actually is, what processes it entails and what its purpose is.' He highlights that people often perceive assessment as a 'stand-alone detached activity'. This is of course the case in many other situations in life, such as a driving test or a hearing test; however assessment in the early years is an ongoing continuous observation process that takes into consideration the child's daily activities, behaviours and achievements in order to inform planning.

- Sancisi and Edington (2015) explain that in order to be reliable and accurate, assessment must be 'based primarily on the practitioner's knowledge of the child gained predominantly from observation and interaction in a range of daily activities and events.'

The two types of assessment are discussed below:

- **Formative assessment** (also known as ongoing assessment) 'involves practitioners observing children to understand their level of achievement, interests and learning styles, and to then shape learning experiences for each child reflecting those observations.' (EYFS, 2017)

- **Summative assessment** summarises the child's learning up to a particular point in time and 'brings together all the formative assessment on a child in a short report and should include information on how the child is developing.' (Soni, 2013)

What is planning?
- Planning in the EYFS is when practitioners draw on the knowledge about a child to ensure that activities and tasks target the next steps in each of the areas of learning and development, taking into consideration the key characteristics of learning for each child. This is all based on the ongoing observation and assessment of each and every child.

Involving parents in the observation, assessment and planning cycle

All parents are keen to know how their child is getting on when they are in the care of other people throughout the day. Parents of EAL learners will be particularly curious about how their child is managing in this new language environment.

Through regular observations of your key children in a range of situations, you will be in a great position to speak confidently to parents about not only what the child has been doing, but also highlighting any areas of progress. For example, if you have observed an EAL learner interacting with other children for the first time, parents would be pleased to hear about this. Similarly, if a child has attempted to use some English words, this would also be of interest to many parents.

Chapter Seven Observation, assessment and planning

The conversations that you have with parents week after week will also play a part in your overall understanding of what each child is capable of. These conversations are particularly important when considering the skills, abilities and learning styles of the EAL learners in your setting, and finding out what they do at home. If they are going through a silent period or if they have not yet developed the confidence to interact with others and participate fully in all activities, this information is vital.

Assessment requirements

Practitioners are required to review each child's progress and share a summative assessment of each child's learning and development at two points during the EYFS. A summative assessment is statutory between the ages of 24 and 36 months (2 year check) and also at the end of the EYFS.

2 Year Check

Settings are required to pull together all of their observations and assessment of children in the three prime areas of learning and development for each child's 2 year check.

> ### What does the EYFS say?
>
> 'When a child is aged between two and three, practitioners must review their progress, and provide parents and/or carers with a short written summary of their child's development in the prime areas.'
>
> 'This progress check must identify the child's strengths, and any areas where the child's progress is less than expected.'
>
> 'If there are significant emerging concerns, or an identified special educational need or disability practitioners should develop a targeted plan to support the child's future learning and development involving parents and/or carers and other professionals (for example, the provider's Special Educational Needs Co-ordinator (SENCO) or health professional(s) as appropriate.'
>
> (EYFS, 2017)

For children who are learning English as an additional language, it is essential to comment on their understanding and use of English within the setting and also evaluate their progress in learning when they are using their home language. To facilitate this, it is useful when recording any observations of an EAL learner to make a note of the language used by the adult and by the child in the situation, if appropriate.

'Practitioners must discuss with parents and/or carers how the summary of development can be used to support learning at home.' (EYFS, 2017) This is the perfect opportunity to ensure that parents have a good understanding of what they can do at home to support their child's communication and language development. See page 70 for advice that you can give to parents regarding supporting language development at home.

If there are concerns about a child's development in any of the prime areas, a targeted plan to help the child develop in these areas must be discussed with parents and, if applicable, any professionals who work with the child.

Chapter Seven Observation, assessment and planning

Case study: 2 year check

Child's name: Madeline
Child's age: 2 years, 3 months
Background information: Madeline has been learning English and French since birth as her dad is English and her mum is French. She started attending a private nursery at 18 months of age. The summary of her learning and development that was written by practitioners for Madeline's 2 year check indicated that she was progressing well in each of the prime areas (communication and language, personal, social and emotional development and physical development). Staff commented that Madeline has strong skills in personal, social and emotional development, as she is very keen on interacting with the other children and she is making really good progress with learning to share and take-turns with the other children.

Parent perspective

Both of Madeline's parents attended her 2 year check meeting.
Her father said:
"It was so useful to hear about how Madeline is doing at nursery. I am very pleased with her progress and I am happy that she plays nicely with the other children. Madeline's key person is fantastic; she always makes sure Madeline is ok. Madeline will be moving to a different nursery soon as we are moving house, so it is useful to have all of this information to take with us."

Assessment at the end of the EYFS

At the end of the EYFS, practitioners are required to decide whether or not each child has met each of the early learning goals, based on their ongoing observation and assessment.

You must also evaluate each child's progress in the four other areas of learning: mathematics, literacy, expressive arts and design, understanding the world, in addition to the three prime areas that underpin children's core development. For children learning EAL, along with a main focus on nurturing communication and building confidence, you need to find out how well children can count and manipulate numbers, how they respond to music, what they know about the world and how their imagination works!

In terms of assessment, the statutory requirement specifies no differences in the way monolingual children and EAL learners are assessed. It does however state that the early learning goals for language and communication and also for literacy must be assessed in English for all children (EAL requirement 4), yet the outcomes of the other early learning goals can be assessed in any language.

So, if a child is counting or naming shapes in his home language, you would of course record this and use this to inform the summative assessment. Depending on whether any practitioners in the setting can speak the same language as the child, a parent may need to be consulted regarding the names of the shapes or how to count in the home language and discuss how well the child shows they can do this when in their home environment. Alternatively, the internet can be used (e.g. programmes and games in the child's home language) to gather this information, or an interpreter can support and talk with the child in the home language about the shapes, for example, and then feedback to you. Having dual-language maths resources would also be helpful to support the child to flourish in this specific area of learning and development.

What does the EYFS say?

'Each child's level of development must be assessed against the early learning goals.'

'Practitioners must also complete a short commentary of each child's skills and abilities in relation to the three characteristics of learning.'

'When assessing communication, language and literacy skills, practitioners must assess children's skills in English.' (EYFS, 2017) This is to ensure that children are 'ready to benefit from the opportunities available to them when they begin Year 1.'

(EYFS, 2017)

Chapter Seven Observation, assessment and planning

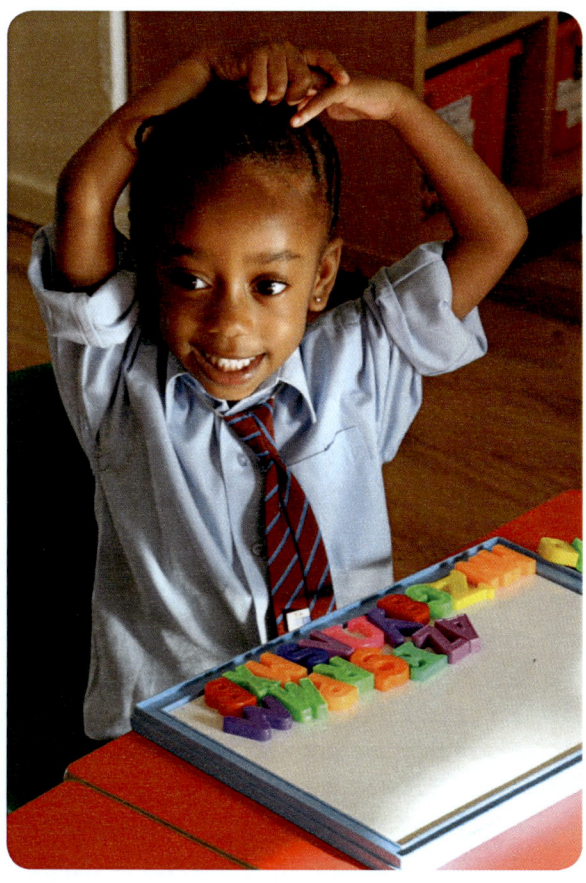

a good standard in English language during the EYFS' (EYFS, 2017). However, you may get some children who start at your setting towards the end of the EYFS and who may have little or no English. Even for these children, their abilities in each of the early learning goals for communication and language and literacy must be based on their skills in English.

You may have children who have good communication and language skills in their home language, but are not yet able to meet the early learning goals for communication and language in English. Soni (2013) highlights that 'it is more likely that children who have learned English sequentially are below their monolingual peers when assessed at the end of the Reception year. This is because it can take up to two to three years to be fluent in a new language and more than five years to use the cognitive and academic aspects of the language effectively.' (Soni, 2013)

'If a child does not have a strong grasp of English language, practitioners must explore the child's skills in the home language with parents and/or carers, to establish whether there is cause for concern about

For each of the early learning goals, 'practitioners must judge whether a child is meeting the level of development expected at the end of Reception year (expected), exceeding this level (exceeding) or not yet reaching this level (emerging).' (Soni, 2013)

Levels of development

Emerging – the child has not yet demonstrated this skill consistently in a range of situations.

Expected – the child has demonstrated this skill on multiple occasions within a range of situations.

Exceeding – the child has very good mastery of this skill and has actually demonstrated skills and abilities above this early learning goal, which are therefore above the expected skill level for a child of their age.

This book emphasises the importance of ensuring that all children have 'sufficient opportunities to learn and reach

Chapter Seven Observation, assessment and planning

language delay.' (EYFS, 2017) See pages 89-90 for information and advice about how best to explore a child's skills in their home language and how to establish whether or not there is cause for concern.

Below is an example of part of an EYFS profile:
The above excerpt of an EYFS profile shows a child's

Early Learning Goals

Prime Area: Communication and Language	
Listening and attention • Children can listen attentively in a range of situations. They listen to stories accurately anticipating key events and respond to what they hear with relevant comments, questions or actions. They give their attention to what others say and respond appropriately, while engaged in another activity.	Expected
Understanding • Children follow instructions involving ideas or actions. They answer 'how' and 'why' questions about their experiences and in response to stories and events.	Expected
Speaking • Children express themselves effectively, showing awareness of listeners' needs. They use past, present and future tenses accurately when talking about events that have happened or are to happen in the future. They develop their own narratives and explanations by connecting ideas or events.	Emerging

outcomes for each of the early learning goals in the prime area of communication and language. The child has achieved the expected level for both listening and attention and understanding, however they have not fully achieved the expected level for speaking.

When sharing a child's EYFS profile with parents and discussing any areas that a child has not achieved 'expected' for, practitioners should reassure parents by explaining how the child can be supported in this area at home.

Bear in mind that the younger children in Reception (i.e. those born in the summer months) can be almost a year younger than the older children in the year group. This is likely to be reflected in the attainment of these younger children, as they have not had as long to develop their skills and reach the early learning goals. When appropriate, make sure parents understand this when discussing the outcomes of goals for the youngest children in your setting.

Short written commentary

As well as stating the child's attainment in relation to each of the early learning goals, a written summary about the child's skills and abilities is required, in relation to the three key characteristics of effective learning.

As a result of the continuous observation, assessment, planning cycle, you will have a wealth of knowledge about each child by this stage. Remember that parents and carers remain crucial in contributing to this EYFS profile.

The EYFS framework states that the EYFS profile 'must reflect: ongoing observation; all relevant records held by the setting; discussions with parents and carers, and any other adult whom the teacher, parent or carer can offer a useful contribution.' (EYFS, 2017)

For each of the key characteristics of learning, think about examples of times when the child has demonstrated each of these. For example, when considering the first characteristic of learning 'playing and exploring', can you think of times when the child has made discoveries through exploration. For example, they may have found out how many legs spiders have during a mini beast hunt.

They may have shown a willingness to 'have a go' during a fruit tasting activity where they tried a range of new foods, or they may have attempted to climb up the climbing frame using the rope for the first time.

Combine your own examples with any additional information that parents may have provided about the child's learning and development outside of your setting.

This written commentary acts as an incredibly useful overview for staff members who will be supporting the children when they progress into Year 1.

Chapter Seven Observation, assessment and planning

Case Study: EYFS profile

Child's name: Bilal
Child's age: 4 years, 7 months
Home language: Urdu

Bilal was born in Pakistan. He and his family moved to the UK when he was almost 18 months old. Bilal was first properly exposed to English when he started Reception.

Bilal's EYFS profile indicated that he was either 'expected' or 'exceeding' in all of the early learning goals in areas of physical development and mathematics.

However, his attainment in all of the communication and language early learning goals were agreed to be 'emerging' based on his abilities in English. He experiences difficulties expressing himself in English and he also struggles to follow instructions and answer questions.

Practitioners have observed that, when interacting with the other children in the setting who also speak his home language, Bilal is able to express himself and engage in full conversations.

When discussing the outcomes of the early learning goals with Bilal's mother, his class teacher highlighted that Bilal is still in the early stages of learning English which is why he has not met the early learning goals in relation to language and communication.

Bilal's mother reported that she was considering stopping speaking Urdu to Bilal at home to focus on his English. Bilal's class teacher emphasised the important role that Urdu plays in learning for Bilal, and strongly advised that parents continue to expose him to Urdu at home.

In summary, when supporting EAL learners in your setting, there is often an early focus on the prime area of PSED to set the foundation for future language and communication development. For these children, getting a real understanding of 'how' they learn will help you to see what they are really capable of and to ensure that their abilities and skills are not underestimated.

Of course, all of the EYFS requirements must be followed, which includes summative assessments at 2 years as well as at the end of the EYFS. Assessment in five of the areas of learning and development (maths, expressive arts and design, understanding the world, physical development and PSED) can be based on skills that a child has demonstrated in any language. Each child's abilities in relation to the early learning goals for language and communication and literacy must be assessed in English.

In the whole observation, assessment and planning cycle, working in partnership with parents helps practitioners to gain a true insight into the child's abilities, particularly when they are speakers of more than one language.

Chapter Eight Working with children with communication difficulties

The ability to communicate effectively is a must have skill for all. By the end of the EYFS, children are expected to be able to: express themselves effectively while showing awareness of their listeners' needs, use past, present and future tenses accurately, develop their own narratives, answer 'how' and 'why questions, follow instructions and respond to what they hear with relevant comments, questions or actions. (EYFS, 2017)

However, for some children, developing skills in this prime area of learning and development is a challenge. There are many different types of communication difficulties that can make it hard for children to meet these early learning goals. This chapter explores the term SLCN, which stands for speech, language and communication needs.

As an early years practitioner you are likely to have come across children with speech, language and communication needs (SLCN) as it is estimated that around 10% children have a communication difficulty (The Communication Trust, 2011).

There is a wide range of different types of speech, language and communication difficulties and no two children with SLCN difficulties are the same.

Children who are new to English must not be classed as a having a communication difficulty or a special educational need or disability on the basis that they speak a different language. If a child is an EAL learner, this does not mean that the child has SLCN. What's

Chapter Eight Working with children with communication difficulties

more, being exposed to more than one language does not cause children to have SLCN or special educational needs and disabilities. (RCSLT, 2006)

'Learning English as an additional language is not a special educational need.' (DfE, 2013)

It has already been highlighted that many children start school each year with communication difficulties, a figure that is thought to reach up to 50% of children in areas of deprivation (The Communication Trust, 2011). Bearing in mind the fact that some settings (particularly in and around London) cater for high numbers of children whose first language is not English, we can conclude that those settings will be supporting children who are EAL learners and who also have a communication difficulty of some sort.

Winter (1999) found that 59% of Speech and Language Therapists working with children in England had at least one bilingual child on their caseload. 11% of therapists had twenty or more bilingual children on their caseload (Winter, 1999).

EAL learners are no more likely than monolingual children to have SLCN, however research suggests that when they do have such difficulties, they are more likely to be missed and not identified. (ICAN, 2007)

The impacts of SLCN can be devastating if not identified and addressed in childhood. The Communication Trust's research between 2009 and 2016 highlights that those with communication and language difficulties are at greater risk of literacy difficulties, social isolation, low self-esteem and challenging behaviour. If unresolved, adults with communication and language difficulties are more likely to experience unemployment, mental health difficulties and crime-related police involvement. Ensuring that the right support is in place for children with SLCN in the early years is essential to ensure that these children don't go on to face the difficulties mentioned above.

As it can be harder to identify SLCN in children learning EAL, it is key that practitioners have a good understanding of typical additional language acquisition (see Chapter two), as well as knowledge of the types of communication needs that children can experience.

As well as exploring the different types of communication difficulties that a child can experience, this chapter also discusses what you can do if you are concerned about a child's development in the prime area of language and communication and how to ensure that you are meeting the requirements set out in the EYFS (EAL requirement 5).

This chapter also explores how you, as early years practitioners, can identify EAL learners who are experiencing SLCN and of course how to support these children within your setting.

The chapter is split into three parts:

1) Understanding SLCN

2) Identifying SLCN in EAL learners

3) Supporting EAL learners with SLCN.

Chapter Eight Working with children with communication difficulties

Understanding Speech, Language and Communication Needs (SLCN)

Speech, Language and Communication

The three terms speech, language and communication are each discussed separately below:

Language
Language encompasses receptive and expressive language skills.
- **Receptive language** is the ability to understand what someone else is saying. It is 'the ability to understand words and sentences so that we can follow what is being said to us.' (Elks and McLauchlan, 2016)
- **Expressive language** is the ability to use words to express oneself. 'It involves organising our thoughts and ideas using appropriate vocabulary into grammatically correct sentences ready for talking.' (Elks and McLauchlan, 2016)

Speech
This refers to the physical process of producing speech sounds and saying words. It is 'how we articulate sounds and combine sounds to say words.' (Elks and McLauchlan, 2016)

Communication
This is a broad term that includes speech and language skills. It also includes 'the ability to understand and use gesture, body language, facial expression, our voice and situational clues to help communicate our message.' (Elks and McLauchlan, 2016)

The Communication Chain

Elks and McLachlan (2015) developed the 'communication chain' shown below, to demonstrate the processes that we have to go through in order to communicate. Many of the processes on the chain are interlinked with one another.

If an individual has difficulties with one area in the communication chain, this often has a knock on effect

Chapter Eight Working with children with communication difficulties

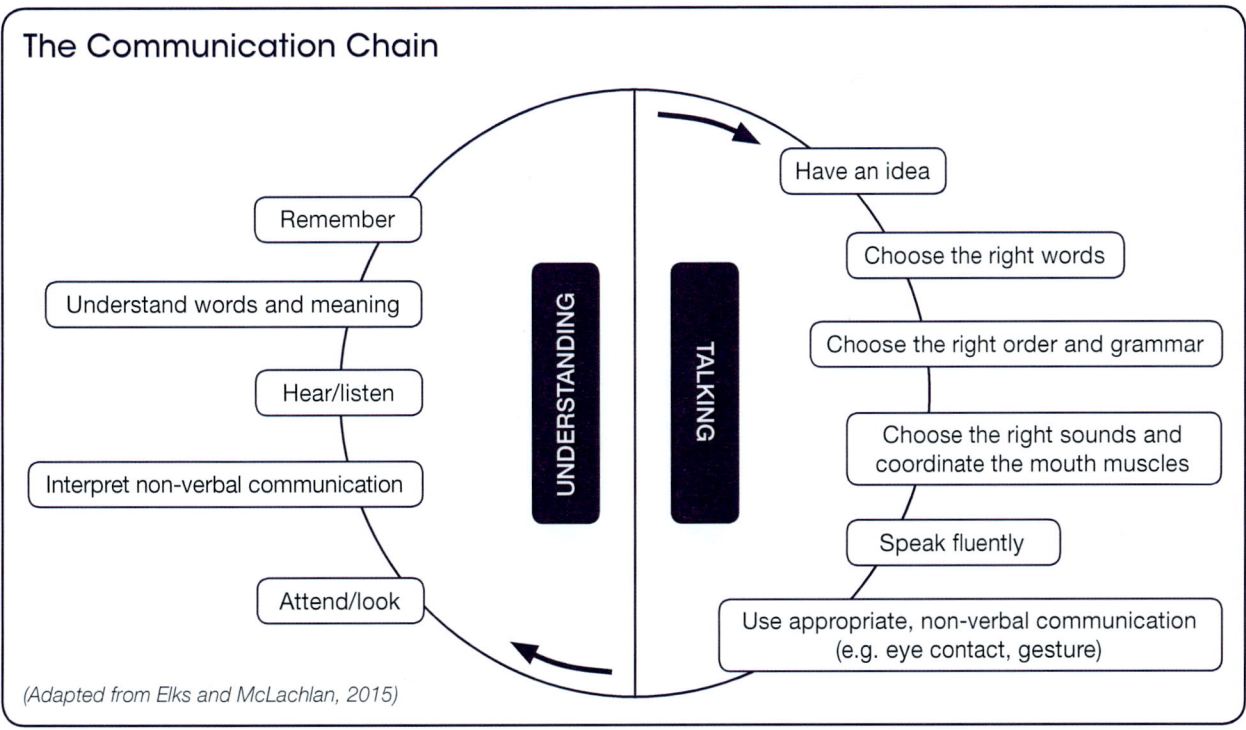

(Adapted from Elks and McLachlan, 2015)

on one or more of the other areas. For example, if a child has difficulties with attention, which is right at the start of the communication chain, this can cause them to experience difficulties with understanding language and using language, as it can act as a barrier to learning these skills.

We know that receptive language skills (understanding language) are usually in advance of expressive language skills (using words), therefore children who have difficulties with the skills on the left side of the chain will typically also experience difficulties with the skills on the right side of the chain.

In order to communicate effectively, a person needs to have good receptive language skills (understanding of the language) and good expressive language skills (ability to use words to communicate an intended message). They also need to be able to communicate in an appropriate way which involves reading the non-verbal communication of others and amending their communication based on the responses of others.

Effective communication also involves being able to speak in a fluent way and being able to pronounce the words in a way that other people can understand.

During the early years children are continuing to develop their skills in each of the above areas and by the end of Reception, children are expected to have good mastery of these skills. However for some children, developing the skills to be able to communicate effectively is a real challenge, whether they are exposed to one language or more than one language.

Different types of SLCN

Below are some of the communication difficulties that you may encounter in your work with early years children:

Receptive language difficulties
- Some children struggle to understand what is being said to them.
- They may struggle to understand the meaning of individual words that we say as well as struggling to understand whole instructions or questions that we ask them.
- These children struggle to meet the receptive language milestones outlined in the table on page 22.
- Children with receptive language needs often rely on non-verbal communication or contextual cues. For example, when we ask them to get their coats on, we might point to the coats or hold up a coat, so even if a child is not able to understand the instruction given

Chapter Eight Working with children with communication difficulties

(the words) they can often still follow the instruction by looking at our body language and the context (for example, all of the other children putting their coats on).
- These children also often copy the behaviours of other children, therefore it can be a challenge to identify them as having a communication difficulty, as they can appear to understand the instructions we give them.

Expressive language difficulties
- Some children have difficulties using words and spoken language effectively.
- They may have a smaller vocabulary than other children of their age.
- They may struggle to join words together.
- They may struggle to apply grammatical rules when talking.
- These children struggle to meet many of the expressive language milestones shown in the table on page 22.

Delayed language skills
- Many toddlers have 'a simple delay in language, i.e. their language is following a normal pattern but at a slower rate.' (Elks & McLauchlan, 2016)

- For example, they may not say their first words until 2 years of age, of they may not be able follow the instructions that other children of their age can follow.
- Children with delayed language skills might have delayed skills in both receptive language (understanding) and expressive language (use of language) or perhaps just with expressive language.

Developmental Language Disorder
- Developmental Language Disorder (DLD) is a condition where children experience difficulties understanding and/or using spoken language.
- Children with Developmental Language Disorder often have a combination of strengths and areas of need that are not usually seen in typical language development.
- For example, they may have a good vocabulary and know a lot of words, however, they may struggle to get the words in the right order, or they may miss out important grammatical words.
- No two children with Developmental Language Disorder are the same.

Social communication difficulties
- Some children have difficulties interacting with peers.
- They may struggle to understand and follow the social rules of communication and may also find it hard to interpret the non-verbal communication of others, such as facial expressions.
- Children with social communication difficulties find it hard to interact with others appropriately.
  They may have greater difficulties than most children their age with the following:
  - Turn-taking
  - Knowing what might upset someone else
  - Interpreting the facial expressions and body language of someone else
  - Using appropriate facial expressions and body language
  - Knowing how close to get to others (proximity)
  - Making and maintaining friendships.
- Children with typically developing communication skills gradually improve their skills in each of the above throughout the early years. They might not be perfect at all of these things by the end of the EYFS, for example, they may still need support to share and take turns at times. However, for children with social communication difficulties, the above skills don't come naturally and they need more support to develop these skills.

Chapter Eight Working with children with communication difficulties

Autism Spectrum Disorder
- Autism is 'a lifelong developmental disability that affects how a person communicates with and relates to other people, and how they experience the world around them.' (autism.org.uk)
- For many years, statistics have shown that more than 1 in 100 people receive a diagnosis of Autism Spectrum Disorder (autism.org.uk). However recent research suggests that autism is actually far more common than this. (Baio, Wiggins, Christensen, et al., 2018)
- Individuals with autism typically experience difficulties with social communication and social interaction. In addition, they typically present with 'restricted, repetative patterns of behaviour, interests or activities.' (DSM-5, 2013)
- As the name suggests, the condition is a 'spectrum' which means that it can vary in severity. Some children with autism are able to develop very good language skills, whereas other children with autism do not develop the ability to communicate using words. This shows how different individuals with autism can be.

Attention and listening difficulties
- Some children struggle to pay attention to activities and listen to others.
- They may move very quickly from one activity to the next and rarely complete a task.
- They may not respond to their name or to verbal instructions.
- They may appear to be 'always on-the-go', more so than the other children of the same age.
- Attention and listening difficulties often have an impact on a child's language development. This is because these children struggle to listen to others which makes it harder for them to pick up language.

Some children develop good language skills and good social communication skills, however they struggle with other aspects of communication, such as pronouncing sounds accurately or getting their words out fluently.

These children may achieve all of communication and language early learning goals, however they may nevertheless require specific support to help with the aspect of communication that they are struggling with (e.g. speech sounds).

Speech sound difficulties
- Be aware that different speech sounds typically develop at different ages, as some sounds are more difficult to pronounce than others. A child aged 2 years and 6 months is likely to be able to pronounce sounds including b, p, m, n, d, however they may not be able to pronounce sh, j or z.
- Some children have difficulties pronouncing certain sounds that other children their age have mastered. This can make it difficult for them to make themselves understood.
- Some children are simply not meeting expected milestones in speech sound development (delay) whereas other children's speech does not follow the expected pattern of speech sound development (disorder).

Stammering
- Some children have difficulties getting their words out fluently and their speech is hesitant.
- There are a range of different stammering behaviours including:
  - Stretching out a sound (e.g. mmmmmmummy)
  - Repeating a single sound (e.g. d..d..d…daddy)
  - Repeating whole words (e.g. but…but…but…)
  - Not being able to get anything out at all.

  Some children who stammer do all of the above, whereas other children just do one or two.
- Sometimes children who stammer may also have certain physical behaviours that accompany their stammer (e.g. they may clench their fists, or screw up their face when trying to get words out).

Other conditions
Some children experience speech, language and communication difficulties as a result of other conditions. For example, those with cerebral palsy (a condition affecting movement and co-ordination) often experience difficulties with speech as a result.

Similarly, children with learning disabilities will often have language and communication difficulties alongside this.

Some children have more than one of the needs described above. For example, a child may have Autism Spectrum Disorder and also have speech sound difficulties. Alternatively they may have delayed language skills and also have a stammer.

Chapter Eight Working with children with communication difficulties

Identifying SLCN in EAL learners

At times, it can be hard for practitioners to identify whether or not a child who is new to English has a communication difficulty (SLCN). This is particularly true of settings that don't cater for a large number of EAL learners.

The more confident you feel in your knowledge of language and communication development and developmental milestones, the better you should feel about your ability to recognise and identify children who have SLCN. Chapter two outlines the steps that children typically go through when exposed to a new language.

When exposed to a new language after gaining skills in a home language, children will fall into one of the following three groups:

- **Typical additional language acquisition**
  Many EAL learners who have age-appropriate skills in their home language(s) pick up English as a result of good quality interactions with adults and experimentation with the new language when with peers. They will go through many of the steps highlighted on page 25, which may or may not include a silent period.

- **Difficulties acquiring a new language**
  Some children find it difficult to learn English as an additional language, despite having no difficulties with their first language. These children may remain in the silent period for longer than expected and they may need additional support to learn English.

- **Difficulties in the home language and therefore difficulties acquiring a new language (SLCN)**
  There are also some EAL learners who have difficulties developing skills in their home language. For these children, acquiring and being able to communicate effectively in English as an additional language can be even more of a challenge.

In order to establish whether a child has SLCN rather than difficulties solely with learning an additional language, it is essential to have a clear understanding of what the child's language skills are like in their strongest language.

Chapter Eight Working with children with communication difficulties

The Statutory Framework (2017) states that 'If a child does not have a strong grasp of English language, practitioners must explore the child's skills in the home language with parents and/or carers, to establish whether there is cause for concern about language delay.' (EAL requirement 5)

Exploring the child's skills in their home language

You will hopefully have explored the child's abilities in their home language(s) in some detail with parents at the pre-start information sharing meeting, however the amount of information gained from parents at this point will of course vary, and there may be instances where this discussion did not take place before the child joined the setting.

If a child is not able to use English and you do not have information about their language skills in their home language, arrange a time to meet with the parents to discuss this.

Ask about the child's abilities in the child's home language and at what age they started using words (if they are using words) and compare these to the milestones shown on page 22. For example, if a child who is 3 and a half years old is using single words at home and said his first words after the age of 2 years, we can see from the table on page 22 that he is not meeting the developmental milestones for his age.

In the resources section on page 106, there is a checklist that will help you to ask the right kind of questions and to check where the child is at in his or her home language.

The information that the parent gives you will hopefully allow you to have a good idea of whether or not the child has developed skills that are typical for his or her age in the home language. However, you may find that some parents will find it difficult to give you this information. Also, parents themselves will have their own attitudes towards the child's development in language and communication and may be either completely happy with the child's development or concerned.

If both you and the child's parent(s) have concerns about the child's speech, language and communication development in the home language after considering developmental milestones, the child could indeed have SLCN. For these children, it would be appropriate for them to access a Speech and Language Therapy assessment for more support and guidance. Page 92 has more information about Speech and Language Therapy and access to this.

However, in some cases, parents will not be concerned about their child's language and communication skills, when in fact the child is not meeting developmental milestones in this prime area. This occurs for a whole host of reasons; many parents aren't aware of the development milestones for language and communication. Alternatively, many parents have other priorities, for example if the child has a health condition, the child's health would be the priority, or for families who are refugees, they may be dealing with other important family circumstances, such as sorting out poor housing or applying for permanent residency status, for example.

The EYFS states that 'Practitioners must consider whether a child may have a special educational need or disability which requires specialist support. They should link with, and help families to access, relevant services from other agencies as appropriate.' (EYFS, 2017)

If you have a concern about the language and communication skills of an EAL learner that parents haven't raised, take a look at the section below and take all of these factors into consideration. For example, if you are concerned with how the child interacts (or doesn't interact) with the other children in your setting, it is important to give the child some time to settle before jumping to any conclusions about a child having SLCN. Children who are new to English are likely to be experiencing a range of emotions as previously discussed and there are also cultural differences to consider. Remember that the silent period is also typical for children who are new to a language.

The way in which you would approach raising concerns with parents will depend on a whole host of factors, particularly as there are so many different types of speech, language and communication needs. Whenever discussing concerns about a child, try to do so out of the earshot of the child. Perhaps another staff member could play with the child while conversations of this nature are happening. Also, always make a conscious effort to highlight some positives whenever discussing a child with his or her parents.

Chapter Eight Working with children with communication difficulties

If you have noticed that a child in your setting appears to be stammering when trying to speak, it would be appropriate to speak to parents about this as soon as possible. They might have noticed that their child does this at home too. With stammering, the evidence shows that the earlier a child accesses therapeutic intervention (Speech and Language Therapy) for a stammer, the greater the likelihood that the stammer will go away (Stewart, 2016).

It is not uncommon for practitioners to believe that a child has a communication difficulty, however when their linguistic and cultural background is looked into a little more closely, it turns out that they do not in fact have a communication difficulty at all and what they are doing is very typical of a child in their situation who is in a new language environment.

The way in which children learn an additional language when exposed to this language after the age of around 3 years, is different to the acquisition of their first language.

As an early years practitioner in a setting that caters for EAL learners, it is useful to know the steps that children typically go through when exposed to a new language. See page 25 for an outline of the stages that children typically go through when exposed to a new language. Having some knowledge about how children typically acquire new languages should make it easier to identify when an EAL learner has SLCN.

Below are several reasons that can make it difficult to identify whether an EAL learner has SLCN:

Cultural differences

It is important to be aware that there are cultural differences in some aspects of communication, particularly when it comes to social communication norms, such as the use of eye contact. For example, if a child comes from a culture where people consider it to be rude to make direct eye contact, the child may rarely look you or others in the eye. It is therefore important to consider the customs of the child's culture if there are concerns with social communication.

> *'Social communication behaviours such as eye contact, facial expressions, and body language, are influenced by sociocultural and individual factors.'* (www.asha.org)

Also, children who are new to English may not get involved with other children as readily as the children in your setting who have full command of the English language.

Attention and listening in an unfamiliar language environment

Remember, 'when a young child is learning a new language it is demanding and tiring. Their level of concentration will be affected. They will be more able to listen and attend in an environment using their home language.' (Elks and Mclachlan, 2016)

It is important to differentiate children who are simply becoming tired and restless due to the exposure of the new language from children who actually have attention and listening difficulties. Children who are new to a language will tire easily; they can only maintain their focus on the new language for short periods at a time.

Chapter Eight Working with children with communication difficulties

They may appear to have 'switched off' during group time input at times. This is typically due to the high demands that are placed on them throughout the day in the new language environment.

EAL learners 'whose English language skills are not yet adequate for the learning demands' of the setting may present with 'a short attention span, especially if the topic is unfamiliar.' (naldic.org.uk)

Differences in the sounds of the language

It is also important to remember that there are some sounds that occur in some languages and not others. So EAL learners who speak a language that does not make use of all of the sounds that occur in the English language may struggle to pronounce the sounds that don't exist in their home language. For example, a child who speaks Gujarati may struggle to pronounce words that contain the 'w' sound as this sound is not used in this language.

Case Study: attention and listening skills

Child's name: Yasir
Child's age: 3 years, 4 month
Background information: Yasir has lived in the UK since birth. However, he was first exposed to English properly when he started nursery shortly after turning 3 years of age.

His key person noticed that he was able to participate in child-led activities for quite lengthy periods of time. However, he struggled to sit and listen during group time. Yasir's mum reported that he is able to sit and listen to several stories in a row at home when their home language of Arabic is used.

The nursery staff understand that it is hard for Yasir to pay attention and listen for more than a few minutes at a time when English is being spoken, as he is not yet familiar with this language.

They have taken a number of steps to support Yasir:
- They now make group input time more active
- They use Signalong signs as much as possible when talking, as Yasir seems to find it easier to listen and understand what is being said when signs are used
- They try to include Yasir's interests of superheroes and dinosaurs into activities when possible
- They have rearranged the carpet seating spots so that Yasir is now next to children who have good attention and listening skills
- They make a conscious effort to look out for any signs that Yasir may need a break or some movement.

Since the nursery staff made these changes, they have noticed that Yasir is now able to sit and listen for slightly longer. They have also noticed that his English is improving.

Chapter Eight Working with children with communication difficulties

Supporting EAL learners with speech, language and communication needs

'Research shows that when parents and carers work together they can positively affect the language development of children under 5 years.' (Elks and McLauchlan, 2016)

This section looks at how you can support EAL learners in your setting who have speech, language and communication needs in your everyday practice, as well as discussing Speech and Language Therapy support for children.

Speech and Language Therapy

Speech and Language Therapists are health professionals who work with individuals who have speech, language and communication needs, as well as those with eating and drinking difficulties.

How do Speech and Language Therapists help children?

The way Speech and Language Therapists support children depends on the kind of difficulties that each individual child experiences. A different type of support would be given to a child who is delayed in reaching language milestones, compared to a child who has a stammer or a child who has difficulties pronouncing certain speech sounds.

For children in the early years, therapy sessions are only a very small part of what is going to help them make progress. Speech and Language Therapists also usually give parents/carers and others working with the child advice, support and often activities that they can do at home or within a setting to support the child.

This is because the people who are with the children on a daily basis play an absolutely crucial part in supporting their communication development.

Chapter Eight Working with children with communication difficulties

Access to Speech and Language Therapy services

In some areas, there is an open referral process and anyone can refer a child for an assessment, including parents, carers and practitioners. In other areas, a GP referral is required. Many services have a certain criteria that a child has to meet in order to access Speech and Language Therapy services.

There may be children in your setting who are accessing Speech and Language Therapy. If you have been sent any reports by the therapist, there may be a range of ideas and strategies that you can use in your setting to support the child. Parents may be able to give you a copy of the child's report if you haven't received one.

If any children in your setting are attending Speech and Language Therapy sessions, having an understanding of what the child is working on in sessions can enable you to support them with the same things in your early years setting. This is what can really make a difference for the child.

Case Study: Speech and Language Therapy

Child's name: Dawid
Child's age: 3 years, 6 months
Background information: Dawid is from a Polish speaking family. He has two older siblings who also speak some English at home.

Dawid started nursery when he was 3 years and 2 months old. At the pre-start information sharing meeting, Dawid's mum told Dawid's key person that he had been attending Speech and Language Therapy sessions for the past few months as he has difficulties with expressive language.

Dawid's mum gave a copy of his Speech and Language Therapy report to Dawid's key person and she said she was happy for this to be shared with the other nursery staff members. The nursery staff are following the advice suggested by Dawid's Speech and Langauge Therapist on a daily basis.

Fortunately, there are other children who also speak Polish in the nursery as well as a Polish volunteer. Dawid therefore has lots of opportunities to develop his understanding and use of Polish as well as English in the nursery setting.

The volunteer has also met with Dawid's mum and she is also following the therapist's advice. She is using language that is slightly more advanced than Dawid's so that he can hear good models in Polish.

She also runs a short multi-sensory group everyday with the three Polish children in the setting. Dawid has enjoyed the gloop and the slime during these sessions and he has attempted to use new words in Polish when exploring these different textures.

Everyday support for EAL learners with SLCN in your setting

For all children who are experiencing speech, language and communication needs, the six principles for quality adult-child interaction are key. These are: 1) provide good models, 2) be responsive, 3) be positive, 4) consider the situation,

Chapter Eight Working with children with communication difficulties

5) consider ages and stages, 6) consider individual circumstances (see pages 53 and 54 for more details).

Supporting EAL learners who have difficulties with language (in their home language and English)

- Working closely with parents to ensure that they know how to support their child's language development at home is key.
- Simplify the language that you are using with the child and use visual support to help them understand what you are saying.
- Ensure that you model language at the right level for the child during a range of hands-on, multisensory activities so that the language is meaningful for the child.
- If the child has been seen by a Speech and Language Therapist, follow any advice given.

Supporting EAL learners with attention and listening difficulties

- Due to the fact that it can be challenging to stay focused and listen for long periods of time when learning a new language, 'allowances should be given and appropriate support provided.' (Elks & Mclachlan, 2016)
- 'Reduce distractions and background noise where possible.' (Elks & Mclachlan, 2016)
- Consider the child's interests and motivators so that you can plan activities that are new and exciting for them. Hands-on and multi-sensory activities are fantastic ways to help EAL learners focus for longer.
- Consider the language that you are using with the child in relation to the child's understanding. For a child who is completely new to English, keep your language very simple.
- Accompany instructions with visuals, such as Signalong or Makaton signs, natural gestures or using pictures to show the child what you mean.
- Be realistic in your expectations of how long a child is expected to sit and listen for and respond to any signs that they are giving you to suggest that they are losing focus, perhaps by incorporating a movement break into your group time at this point.
- During group times, position yourself near to children who struggle to focus and listen. This will hopefully make it easier for them to attend to the task without getting distracted by other children and other things around them.
- 'Ready, steady, go activities' can support children with really limited attention to learn to look, listen and wait, as they have to wait until they hear the word 'go' before they act.
- Activities where the child has to listen to something and copy it (e.g. tap sticks) can also really support the attention skills of young children.
- As with all children, using their name to gain their attention is a key strategy.

Supporting EAL learners with social communication difficulties

- It is essentially about giving the child time to settle in and supporting them to feel comfortable and relaxed in your setting.
- All of the advice about helping children to settle-in (Chapter three) will support them to interact socially with others in the setting.
- Modelling appropriate social communication (e.g. greeting others appropriately) can teach them some of the rules of social communication.
- Consider including these children in a regular group session which focuses on social communication skills such as turn-taking, for example.

Chapter Eight Working with children with communication difficulties

Supporting EAL learners with Autism Spectrum Disorder

- Children who are learning English as an additional language who also have Autism Spectrum Disorder are likely to require a different level of support depending on their individual needs.
- Are any other professionals involved with the child? For example, a Speech and Language Therapist or an Occupational Therapist? If so, these professionals may have provided written advice about how best to support the child within your setting. If not, arranging a time to have a conversation with them (with parental consent) about the child's needs and specific strategies to support their needs is crucial. This is because every child with Autism Spectrum Disorder is different and what works for one child might not be the most suitable approach for another child.

Supporting EAL learners who stammer

- It is important to give the child plenty of time to say what they are trying to say.
- Avoid interrupting the child or finishing off the child's sentences. This can be incredibly frustrating for the child.
- The adults around the child should all make an effort to slow down their own speech. This way, the child is likely to also speak more slowly, which can make it easier to be fluent.
- Simplify the language that you are using with the child.
- Reduce the number of questions that you ask the child, instead comment on what the child is doing or looking at. This way, the child is not under any pressure at all to talk, instead they can contribute on their terms.

Supporting EAL learners who have speech sound difficulties

- Remember that some sounds develop later than others as some are more difficult to produce.
- Get down to the child's level and show them that you are listening.
- Model words that the child has struggled with in a positive way, without telling them that they have said the word incorrectly. For example, if the child says 'I like dods', instead of 'I like dogs', you could responds by saying 'You like dogs? Me too!' This acknowledges what the child has said in a positive way whilst also of letting the child hear how the word that they struggled to say is actually pronounced.
- If you really can't understand what the child is saying due to their speech sound difficulties, can they show you what they mean? E.g. they may take you outside to show you the bird that they were trying to tell you about.
- Respond to what the child has said not how the child said it.
- Play listening activities with the child (e.g. sorting items into piles based on the sound that they start with).

In order to best support a child who has any kind of speech, language or communication difficulty, the communication you have with the child's parents or carers is crucial.

Ensuring that all of the significant people in the child's life are working together to support the child collaboratively can make a huge difference.

Resources
Home activity sheets

For children to thrive, they must have endless opportunities to explore, learn and develop whilst interacting with responsive adults. Ward (2013) explains that 'the home environment and parental involvement in learning activities have a substantial influence of the child's attainment in the early years and beyond.' (Ward, 2013)

With technology advancing at an extraordinary rate, it is perhaps even more important than ever that practitioners inspire parents and promote active, hands-on interactive activities between children and their parents or carers.

Perhaps, suggest that parents set aside some time each week to try out the activities within this section. For parents of EAL learners, recommend that they do these activities and games in their home language to support their child's language development at home.

There are five home activity sheets on the next few pages, however the possibilities are endless. As a practitioner or a student with experience in early years, you will no doubt have many ideas of your own. Use the blank home activity sheet and simply write in activities, or make your own sheets up for parents.

Make an effort to chat to parents to see if they managed to do the activities and to see how they went without putting any pressure on them. This regular conversation about home activities can really support the practitioner and parent relationship.

Children who have completed the activities at home will often be keen to talk about their discoveries or even to bring in items to show you! You will probably also hear the children chatting to each other about the activities that they have done at home.

Resources **Home activity sheet - 1**

Make a shaker

You will need:
- A plastic bottle.
- Something to fill the bottle with that will make a noise, e.g. rice, pasta, lentils.

What to do:
- Wash the bottle out.
- Take off any labels.
- Pour your chosen items (e.g. rice or lentils) into the bottle and screw the lid back on.

When you have made your shaker play a range of games with it.
- Shake it to the beat whilst singing your child's favourite songs and nursery rhymes together.
- In your home language, use words such as quiet, loud, slowly, quickly, fast, ready…steady…go!, stop.

Tip:

If you make enough shakers for each family member, you can all have fun making music together!

Have fun talking together in your home language whilst doing this activity.

Resources Home activity sheet - 2

Kim's game

You will need:
- A selection of 6-10 items (e.g. cup, keys, crayon, etc.)
- A blanket or cloth.

What to do:
- Start with three or four items, depending on the age of the child.
- First, talk together about each item.
- Ask questions such as 'what is it used for?' and 'what does it feel like?'.
- Then tell the child that you're going play a game.
- Place them out on a table or the floor.
- Tell them that they need to look at all of the items very carefully and try to remember what is there.
- Then place the cloth or blanket over all of the items and remove one item without the child seeing..
- Pull the blanket away and then ask the child which item has disappeared.
- If they can do this, make it more difficult by starting with more items.

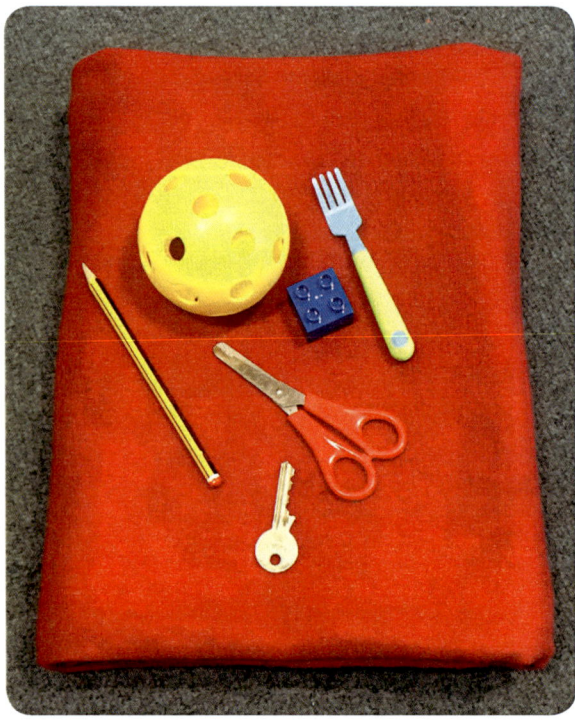

Have fun talking together in your home language whilst doing this activity.

Resources **Home activity sheet - 3**

Photo hunt - outdoors

You will need:
- An outdoor space – either a park or garden!
- This activity sheet and a pencil.

What to do:
- Look at the pictures below together and talk about where you might find each one.
- Hunt for each item and then tick the box when you find it!

Have fun talking together in your home language whilst doing this activity.

Resources Home activity sheet - 4

Photo hunt - home

You will need:
- This activity sheet.
- A pencil.

What to do:
- Look at the pictures below together and talk about where you might find each one.
- Hunt for each item together and then tick the box when you find it! Have fun!

Have fun talking together in your home language whilst doing this activity.

Resources **Home activity sheet - 5**

Fun with ice

You will need:
- Ice cube tray, water and a freezer!
- Small items that the child will be interested in, e.g. lego bricks, miniature toys, etc.

What to do:
- Fill up you ice tray with water and then pop items in with the water. Put this in the freezer.
- When the water freezes, the items will be inside the ice cubes.
- Talk in your home language about how the ice cubes feel using words such as cold, freezing, slippery, smooth.
- Talk about what is happening as the ice melts.
- Talk about the items that are inside the ice cubes.
- Your child could even have a few of these fun ice cubes in the bath with them during bath time.

Have fun talking together in your home language whilst doing this activity.

Resources Home activity sheet

What you need:

What to do:

Tip:

Have fun talking together in your home language whilst doing this activity.

Resources All about me!

All about me!

My name is:

Date of birth:

Home language(s):

I like:

Important people:

Insert photo here

I don't like:

I started learning English...

Other information:

Resources Checklist for pre-start parent meeting

Child's name:	Child's date of birth:

Please comment on your child's general health.
Does your child have any allergies?
Does your child take any medication?
Does your child have any health conditions?
Does your child see any professionals? (e.g. audiologist, paediatrician, etc.)
When did your child last have his/her hearing tested?
What languages are spoken in the home?
What languages do you use when speaking to your child?
If your child has siblings, what language is used between siblings?
Who lives in the home?
Does your child have any siblings? If so, please share names and ages.
If parents are living separately, what contact does your child have with each parent?
Is there anyone else who plays an important part in your child's life?
What religion does the family practice, if any?
Is there anything that we should know about in relation to your child's religion? (e.g. dietary requirements)
How able is your child in the home language(s)?
When did they say their first word(s)? If applicable?

Resources Checklist for pre-start parent meeting

Is your child using words to communicate? Do they join words?
Is your child able to follow instructions at home?
How much exposure has your child had to English?
For how long has your child been exposed to English?
Has your child spent any time in an early years setting or childcare previously?
If so, please give details about previous childcare/early years setting experience (including the name of the setting).
What opportunities has your child had to interact with other children?
Do they enjoy interacting with other children?
How would you describe your child's personality/temperament?
Do you have any concerns about any aspect of your child's development?
Do you have any concerns about your child's eating/drinking?
Is your child toilet trained?
What does your child enjoy doing most? Likes and interests
Can you think of anything that your child does not like doing?
Is there anything else that you would like to share about your child?

Resources Checklist for determining a child's skills in their home language (2 years and over)

Child's name:	Child's date of birth:
When did your child say his or her first words?	
How does your child typically make requests when he / she wants something?	
Can you give some examples of the types of things your child often says?	
Does your child join words together?	
Does your child follow simple instructions in the home?	
Is your child's talking similar to other children of their age?	

Resources
Key words and phrases

Chapter Three focuses on ways in which to prepare for a new starter who is new to the English language. It recommends learning a selection of key words and phrases in the child's home language, whether this is done by asking parents, looking online, or by using the lists on the next few pages for some languages.

When exposed to a new language, children typically attempt to use their home language first, so knowing a few key words and phrases in a child's home language might help you to understand what a child is saying during this period. In addition, you will also be in a better position to give key messages to a child at crucial times or to comfort them when they need it most.

Having a list of words or phrases that you and other practitioners can refer back to when necessary can be really useful. Many parents and carers will be able to tell you some key words and phrases that you can write down. If doing so, remember to make a note of how to pronounce the words too.

The next few pages contain key words and phrases (including a rough pronunciation guide) for some of the most commonly spoken languages in the UK (Polish, Punjabi, Urdu, French).

Remember that each language has its own sound system and many languages contain sounds that don't exist in the English language. For this reason, there are many sounds that are used in different languages that can't be expressed using English spelling. In addition, some languages such as Urdu and Punjabi use a different alphabet system altogether. These factors mean that it is not always easy to accurately note the pronunciation of some words and phrases in other languages.

Resources Key words and phrases - Polish

English	Polish	Rough pronunciation guide
Hello	cześć	chesht
Goodbye	do widzenia	do vidzenya
Good morning	dzień dobry	jen dobre
Good afternoon	n/a	n/a
Yes	tak	tak
No	nie	nyeh
Please	proszę	proshe
Thank you	dziękuję	jen koiya
Good	dobry	dobre
Well done	brawo	bravo
Help	pomocy	pomotze
Dangerous	niebezpieczne	nye beh spetchnye
Careful/be careful	uważaj	uvah jai
It's ok	jest dobrze	yest dobju
Oh dear	ojej	oh yey
Stop	prestań	pshestan
Home	dom	dom
Home time	pora do domu	pora doh domu
Outside	na dwór	na dvor
Water	woda	woda
Toilet	ubikacja / toaleta	ubikatzia
Nappy	pielucha	pieluha
Coat	kurtka	kurtka
Shoes	buty	booteh

Resources Key words and phrases - Punjabi

English	Punjabi	Rough pronunciation guide
Hello	ਸਤ ਸ੍ਰੀ ਅਕਾਲ	sat sri akal
Goodbye	ਅਲਵਿਦਾ	rab rakha
Good morning	ਸਤ ਸ੍ਰੀ ਅਕਾਲ	sat sri akal
Good afternoon	ਸਤ ਸ੍ਰੀ ਅਕਾਲ	sat sri akal
Yes	ਹਾਂ	haa
No	ਨਹੀ	naa
Please	ਕ੍ਰਿਪਾ	kripa
Thank you	ਤੁਹਾਡਾ ਧੰਨਵਾਦ	tuhada dhanavad
Good	ਚੰਗਾ	changa
Well done	ਬਹੁਤ ਖੂਬ	bahoot vadya
Help	ਮਦਦ ਕਰੋ	madad karo
Dangerous	ਖ਼ਤਰਨਾਕ	khatarnak
Careful/be careful	ਸਾਵਧਾਨ	savdhan
It's ok	ਇਹ ਠੀਕ ਹੈ	thika hai
Oh dear	ਓਹ ਪਿਆਰੇ	oh teri / hai ho raba
Stop	ਰੁਕੋ	ruko
Home	ਘਰ	ghar
Home time	ਘਰ ਦਾ ਸਮਾਂ	ghar da sama
Outside	ਬਾਹਰ	bahar
Water	ਪਾਣੀ	pani
Toilet	ਟਾਇਲੈਟ	tati ghar
Nappy	ਨੈਪੀ	langoot
Coat	coat (English word used)	coat (English word used)
Shoes	ਜੁੱਤੀਆਂ	jutia

English as an additional language (EAL) in practice

Resources Key words and phrases - Urdu

English	Urdu	Rough pronunciation guide
Hello	ہیلو	salam walikum
Goodbye	خدا حافظ	khuda aafiss
Good morning	ہیلو	salam walikum
Good afternoon	ہیلو	salam walikum
Yes	جی ہاں	haa
No	نہیں	nahi
Please	براہ کرم	barai karam
Thank you	شکریہ	shukriya
Good	اچھی	aacha
Well done	بہت اچھے	bahut aacha
Help	مدد	madad
Dangerous	خطرناک	katarnak
Careful/be careful	محتاط رہیں	hoshiyar
It's ok	یہ ٹھیک ہے	theek hai
Oh dear	اوہ عزیز	oh mere jaan
Stop	رکھو	ruko
Home	گھر	ghar
Home time	گھر کا وقت	ghar ka waqt
Outside	باہر	bahir
Water	پانی	pani
Toilet	ٹوائلٹ	paa khana
Nappy	n/a	n/a
Coat	coat (the English word is used)	coat (the English word is used)
Shoes	جوتے	jutai

Resources Key words and phrases - French

English	French	Rough pronunciation guide
Hello	bonjour	bonjour
Goodbye	au revoir	oh revoir
Good morning	n/a	n/a
Good afternoon	bonne après-midi	bon aprey-midi
Yes	oui	wee
No	non	noh
Please	s'il vous plaît	si voo play
Thank you	merci	mersee
Good	bien	bien
Well done	bien joué	bien joueh
Help	aidez-moi	aideh mwoh
Dangerous	dangereux	dongeruh
Careful/be careful	prudent	pruden
It's ok	c'est bon	seh bon
Oh dear	oh cher	oh share
Stop	arrêtez	ahreteh
Home	maison	mayzon
Home time	temps à la maison	tom a la mayzon
Outside	à l'extérieur	a lexteriuh
Water	eau	oh
Toilet	toilette	twalet
Nappy	couche	coosh
Coat	manteau	moh too
Shoes	chaussures	shusure

References

Akeci, H., Senji, A., Uibo, H., Kikuchi, Y., Hasegawa, T. & Hietanen, J. (2013) *Attention to eye contact in the West and East: Automatic Responses and Evaluation Ratings.* PLoS ONE 8(3).

American Speech-Language-Hearing Association (ASHA) *Social Communication Disorders in School-Age Children.* Available at: https://www.asha.org/Practice-Portal/Clinical-Topics/Social-Communication-Disorders-in-School-Age-Children/
(Accessed on 5th September 2017)

American Speech-Language-Hearing Association (ASHA). (2013) *Tips for working with an interpreter.* Available at: http://www.asha.org/practice/multicultural/issues/interpret.htm
(Accessed on 22nd July 2017)

Auer, P & Wei, L. (2007) *Handbook of Multilingualism and Multilingual Communication.* Berlin: Walter de Gruyter.

Baio, J., Wiggins, L., Christensen, D. et al. 2018. *Prevalence of Autism Spectrum Disorder Among Children Aged 8 Years.* Autism and Developmental Disabilities Monitoring Network. MMWR Surveillance Summaries. Vol 67, 6.

Beaver, M., Brewster, J., Jones, P., Keene, A., Neaum, S. &Tallack, J. (2002) *Babies and Young Children; Early Years Care and Education.* Cheltenham: Stanley Thornes Ltd.

Blank, J. & Bevan, A. (2017) *Prime Time Communication and Language: An Active Approach to Developing Communication Skills.* London: Practical Pre-School Books.

Blank, J & Mathews, G. (2017) *Prime Time Personal Social and Emotional Development: A Key Person Approach to Learning and Development.* London: Practical Pre-School Books.

Bowen, C. (1998) *Typical Speech and Language Acquisition in Infants and Young Children.* Available at: www.speech-language-therapy.com/
(Accessed on 10th June 2017)

Brodie, K. (2013). *Observation, assessment and planning in the early years. Bringing it all together.* Berkshire: Open University Press.

Brodie, K. & Savage, K. (2015) *Inclusion and Early Years Practice.* London: Routledge.

Brunton, P. & Thornton, L. (2010) *The Parent Partnership Toolkit for Early Years.* London: Optimus Education.

Clarke, P. *Conference Reports:* Creating Positive Environments that Promote Listening and Speaking. Available at: https://www.naldic.org.uk/Resources/NALDIC/Professional%20Development/Documents/Creatingpositiveenvironments.pdf
(Accessed on 23rd September 2017)

Conteh, J. (2015) *The EAL Teaching Book: Promoting Success for EAL Learners.* London: SAGE Publications.

Cote, L. & Bornstein, M. (2015) *Productive vocabulary among three groups of bilingual American children: Comparison and Prediction.* First Language. 34(6): 467-485.

Department for Children, Schools and Families. (2007) *New Arrivals Excellence Programme Guidance.* Norwich: DCSF Publications. Available at: https://www.naldic.org.uk/Resources/NALDIC/Teaching%20and%20Learning/naep.pdf
(Accessed on 16th October 2017)

Department for Children, Schools and Families. (2007) *Primay National Strategy. Supporting children learning English as an additional language.* DCSF Publications. Available at: https://www.naldic.org.uk/Resources/NALDIC/

Teaching%20and%20Learning/ealeyfsguidance.pdf
(Accessed on 6th September 2017)

Department for Education. (2013) *Early Years Foundation Stage Profile Handbook.* DfE. Available at:
www.education.gov.uk/eyfsp
(Accessed on 27th October 2017)

Department for Education. (2012) *Statutory Framework for the Early Years Foundation Stage.* DfE. Available at: http://www.educationengland.org.uk/documents/pdfs/2012-eyfs-statutory-framework.pdf
(Accessed on 9th July 2017)

Department for Education. (2017) *Statutory Framework for the Early Years Foundation Stage.* DfE. Available at: www.gov.uk/government/uploads/system/uploads/attachment_data/file/596629/EYFS_STATUTORY_FRAMEWORK_2017.pdf
(Accessed on 17th June 2017)

Desforges, C. & Arbouchaar, A. (2003) *The Impact of Parental Involvement, Parental Support and Family Education of Pupil Achievement and Adjustment: A Literature Review.* London: Department for Education and Skills in Elks, L & McLachlan, H. 2016. *Early Language Builders*. Cornwall: Elklan.

Dorset Early Years Team. *Children learning English as an additional language (EAL).* Available at: https://www.dorsetforyou.gov.uk/media/pdf/8/4/EAL_in_Early_Years.pdf
(Accessed on 22nd October 2017)

Diagnostic and Statistical Manual of Mental Disorders, 5th Edition. (2013) Arlingtob: American Psychiatric Publishing.

Drury, R. & Robertson, L. (2008) *Strategies for Early Years Practitioners.* Available at: https://www.naldic.org.uk/Resources/NALDIC/Teaching%20and%20Learning/Documents/EYFSStrategies.pdf
(Accessed on 12th September 2017)

Dubeil, J. (2016) *Effective Assessment in the Early Years.* London: Sage Publications.

EAL British Council. *EAL Learners in the UK.* Available at: https://eal.britishcouncil.org/teachers/eal-learners-in-uk)
(Accessed on 8th October 2017)

Early years careers.com. 5 tips to support children with EAL. Available at: http://www.earlyyearscareers.com/eyc/latest-news/5-tips-to-support-children-with-eal/
(Accessed on 15th September 2017)

Eckert, P. & McConnell-Ginet, S. 2013. *Language and Gender.* Cambridge: Cambridge University Press.

Elks, L & McLachlan, H. 2015. *Language Builders*. Cornwall: Elklan.

Elks, L & McLachlan, H. 2016. *Early Language Builders*. Cornwall: Elklan.

Featherstone, S. (2013) *Catching them at it! Assessment in the early years.* London: Featherstone.

Franson, C. (2011) *Bilingualism and Second Language Acquisition.* Naldic. Available at: https://www.naldic.org.uk/eal-teaching-and-learning/outline-guidance/bilingualism/
(Accessed on 21st October 2017)

Gibbons, P. (1991) *Learning to Learn in a Second Language.* Portsmouth: Primary English Teaching Association.

Hayes, C. (2016) *Language, Literacy and Communication in the Early Years: A Critical Foundation.* Northwich: Critical Publishing Ltd.

ICAN (2007) Language and Social Exclusion. I CAN Talk Series – Issue 4. Available at: http://licensing.ican.org.uk/sites/licensing.ican.org.uk/files/Evidence/4_Language_and_Social_Exclusion.pdf
(Accessed on 10th October 2017)

Jarman, E. (2006) *The Communication Friendly Spaces Approach.* Available at:
http://www.elizabethjarmantraining.co.uk/index/php
(Accessed on 10th June 2017)

Literacy Trust (2000) Languages spoken by pupils in London. Available at: www.literacytrust.org.uk/research/lostop3.html
(Accessed on 17th October 2017)

Lyon, J. (1996) *Becoming Bilingual: Language Acquisition in a Bilingual Community.* Clevedon: Cromwell Press.

Macintyre, C & McVitty, K. (2003) *Planning the Pre-5 Setting: Practical Ideas and Activities for the Nursery.* London: Routledge.

MacLeod, A., Fabiano-Smith, L., Boegner-Pagé, S. and Fontolliet, S. (2013) *Simultaneous bilingual language acquisition: The role of parental input on receptive vocabulary development.* Child Lang Teach Ther. 2013 Feb; 29(1).

Madhani. N (1994) *Working with speech and language impaired children from linguistic minority communities.* In Buckley, B. (2003) *Children's Communication: From Birth to Five Years*. London: Routledge.

Maguire-Fong, M. (2015) *Teaching and Learning with infants and toddlers.* New York: Teachers College Press.

Murakami, C. (2008) *'Everybody is Just Fumbling Along': An Investigation of Views Regarding EAL Training and Support Provisions in a Rural Area.* Language and Education Vol. 22, Iss. 4.

Murphy, E. (2011) *Welcoming Linguistic Diversity in Early Childhood Classrooms: Learning from International Schools.* Bristol: Multilingual Matters.

nisra.gov.uk (2011) *Northern Ireland census data, 2011* Available at: https://www.nisra.gov.uk/sites/nisra.gov.uk/files/publications/2011-census-results-key-statistics-statistics-bulletin-11-december-2012.pdf
(Accessed on 27th July 2017)

ons.gov.uk. (2011) *England and Wales census data, 2011* Available at: https://www.ons.gov.uk/peoplepopulationandcommunity/culturalidentity/language/articles/languageinenglandandwales/2013-03-04
(Accessed on 27th July 2017)

Pepper, J. & Weitzman, E. (2004) *It Takes Two to Talk. The Hanen Program.* Ontario: A Hanen Centre Publication.

RCSLT. *What is SLT?* Available at: https://www.rcslt.org/speech_and_language_therapy/docs/factsheets/what_is_slt
(Accessed on 5th September 2017)

RCLST (2006) *Communicating Quality 3*. London: The Royal College of Speech and Language Therapists.

Rizzolatti, G., Fadiga, L., Fogassi, L. & Gallese, V. (2002) *From mirror neurons to imitation: Facts and speculation.* In Meltzoff, A & Prinz, W (2002) *The Imitative Mind: Development Evolution and Brain Bases*. Cambridge: Cambridge University Press.

Rodriguez, R. (2014) *The bilingual advantage. Promoting adacemic development, biliteracy, and native language in the classroom*. Columbia: Teachers College Press.

Roopnarine, J. (2010) *Cultural Variations in Beliefs about Play, Parent-Child Play, and Children's Play: Meaning for Childhood Development.* In Pellegrini, A. (2011) *The Oxford Handbook of the Development of Play.* Oxford: Oxford University Press.

Sancisi, L. & Edington, M. (2015) *Developing High Quality Observation, Assessment and Plannung in the Early Years.* Oxon: Routledge.

Sargent, M. (2016). *100 Ideas for Early Years Practitioners: Supporting EAL learners.* London: Bloomsbury.

Schmidt, M., Pempek, T, Kirkorian, H, Lund, A. & Anderson, D. (2008) *The effects of background television on the toy play behaviour of very young children.* In Spooner, L. & Woodcock, J. (2010) *Teaching Children to Listen: A practical approach to developing children's listening skills.* London: Featherstone.

scotlandcensus.gov.uk. (2011) *Scotland census data, 2011* Available at: http://www.scotlandscensus.gov.uk/documents/censusresults/release2/statsbulletin2.pdf
(Accessed on 27th July 2017)

Sheridan, M. (2008) *From Birth to Five Years: Children's Developmental Progress*. New York: Routledge.

Shopen ,T. (1979) *Languages and their speakers.* Philadelphia: Winthrop Publishers.

Soni, A & Bristow, S. (2012) *The Key Person Approach: How to Support Effective Practice in your Setting.* London: Bloomsbury Publishing.

Soni, A. (2013) *EAL in the Early Years.* London: Featherstone.

Sood, K & Mistry, M. (2015) *English as an Additional Language in the Early Years.* Oxon: Routledge.

Spooner, L. & Woodcock, J. (2013) *Teaching Children to Listen: A practical approach to developing children's listening skills.* London: Featherstone.

TEFL. *Important cultural differences in the classroom.* Available at: https://www.tefl.net/elt/articles/home-abroad/cultural-differences/
(Accessed on 21st September 2017)

Stewart, T. (2016) Stammering: A Resource Book for Teachers. Oxon. Routledge.

The ASHA Leader. (2017) *Handheld Screen Time Linked to Delayed Speech Development* Speech, Voice and Prosodic Disorders. Research in Brief. Vol 22, 16.

The Communication Trust. (2011) *All Together Now.* Available at: www.thecommunicationtrust.org.uk/media/311/all_together_now_v_2.pdf
(Accessed on 14th May 2017)

The National Autistic Society. *What is Autism?* Available at: www.autism.org.uk/about/what-is.aspx
(Accessed on 2nd November 2017)

The National Literacy Trust. (2009) *Press Information.* Available at: www.thecommunicationtrust.org.uk/media/2111/national_campaign_launch_release_-_for_9th_march.pdf
(Accessed on 10th July 2017)

Tomasello, M. (1995) *Beyond Names for Things: Young children's Acquisition of Verbs.* New York: Taylor and Francis Group.

Ward, U. (2013) *Working with Parents in the Early Years.* London: Sage.

Washbourne, A. (2011) *EAL Pocketbook.* London: Management Pocketbooks.

Winter, K. (1999) Speech and Language Therapy Provision for Bilingual Children: Aspects of the Current Service. International Journal of Language and Communication Disorders 34, 1, 85-98.

Acknowledgements

Firstly, thank you to all of the parents and practitioners who were happy to contribute to this book by sharing their thoughts and perspectives. I must also thank the children, parents and staff who feature in the wonderful photographs throughout the book.

A huge thank you to everyone at Rabbsfarm Primary School for being so supportive over the past three years. It has been a pleasure to work with you all and I will miss being part of this lovely team. Thank you also to my wonderful Speech and Language Therapy colleagues in Hillingdon.

I'd like to say a special thank you to Jo Blank for getting me into writing in the first place and also for coming up with so many tips and clever ideas for this book. I really appreciate it all.

My family and closest friends deserve a huge mention. Thank you to my parents for always supporting and encouraging me in everything that I choose to do. I am incredibly grateful. Last but not least, my partner Dan has been a constant source of support with his never-ending patience, encouragement and snacks!

Thank you everyone.